NAVIGATING SCHOOL LIFE: STRATEGIES AND SUPPORT FOR AUTISTIC GIRLS TO TACKLE ACADEMIC, SOCIAL, AND EMOTIONAL CHALLENGES

OVERCOMING SENSORY, EDUCATIONAL, AND SOCIAL BARRIERS IN THE ELEMENTARY SCHOOL YEARS

TAYLOR EBERSTADT

Copyright © 2025 Taylor Eberstadt. All rights reserved.

The content within this book may not be reproduced, duplicated, or transmitted without direct written permission from the author or the publisher.

Under no circumstances will any blame or legal responsibility be held against the publisher or author for any damages, reparation, or monetary loss due to the information contained within this book, either directly or indirectly.

Legal Notice:

This book is copyright-protected. It is only for personal use. You cannot amend, distribute, sell, use, quote, or paraphrase any part of the content within this book without the consent of the author or publisher.

Disclaimer Notice:

Please note the information contained within this document is for educational and entertainment purposes only. All effort has been expended to present accurate, up-to-date, reliable, and complete information. No warranties of any kind are declared or implied. Readers acknowledge that the author is not engaged in the rendering of legal, financial, medical, or professional advice. The content within this book has been derived from various sources. Please consult a licensed professional before attempting any techniques outlined in this book.

By reading this document, the reader agrees that under no circumstances is the author responsible for any losses, direct or indirect, that are incurred as a result of the use of the information contained within this document, including, but not limited to, errors, omissions, or inaccuracies.

ISBN Paperback: 978-0-6486411-7-9

ISBN Hardback: 978-0-6486411-8-6

For inquiries, permissions, or further information, please contact: Taylor@tayloreberstadt.com

CONTENTS

Introduction   7

1. **G: GROWING THROUGH CHALLENGES AT SCHOOL**   13
   What Is Autism and How Does It Impact Girls?   14
   Differences in the Autistic Brain   17
   Autism in Girls   18
   How Does Autism Affect Girls' Learning?   19
   Autism and Learning Disorders   22
   Autism and ADHD   22
   How Learning Disorders Can Affect a Child's Mental Health   23
   Autism and Self-Esteem   23
   Learned Helplessness and Task Avoidance   24
   The Importance of Receiving an Early Diagnosis   26

2. **I: INVESTIGATING SCHOOL OPTIONS**   31
   School Options   32
   Extended School Year (ESY) Services   41
   Tips for Working with Teachers   42

3. **R: ROUTINES THAT FOSTER SUCCESS**   45
   The Elements of a Successful Routine   46
   Tools for Creating a Routine   49
   Setting Up Your Child's Daily Routines   51
   A Note on Sleep   54
   Determining a Healthy Amount of Screen Time for Your Child   55
   Preparing Your Child for Changes to Her Routine   57

4. **L: LEARNING STRATEGIES FOR ACADEMIC GROWTH**   63
   Recognizing Different Learning Styles   64
   The Importance of Differentiated Instruction   65
   VARK Learning Styles and Gardner's Theory of Multiple Intelligences   65
   Sharing Your Child's Special Interests with Teachers   69
   Fostering Your Child's Special Interests Outside School   71

How to Help Your Child Prepare for Tests and
Assessments 71
Helping Your Child Develop a Confident Mindset 74
Special Arrangements for Your Child During Exams 74
Helping Your Child Deal with Setbacks 75

5. ⬢: SENSORY SUCCESS 79
How Sensory Challenges Can Impact Learning 80
Creating a Sensory Map 81
Letting Teachers Know About Your Child's Sensory
Challenges 83
Calming Exercises and Activities 86
Sensory-Friendly Websites and Apps: 91

6. ⬢: SEEKING CONNECTION 97
Social Challenges Faced by Autistic Girls 99
Social Anxiety in Autistic Girls 101
Alexithymia and Autism 102
Friendship Preferences for Autistic Girls 103
Helping Your Daughter Find Her Strawberry People 107
Helping Your Child Find Special Interest Groups 108
Siblings as a Source of Support and Friendship for
Autistic Kids 109

7. ⬢: HARNESSING SMART TECHNOLOGY 113
Tech for Learning 114
Tech for Communication 115
Tech for Tracking Goals and Outcomes 117
Tech for Sensory Challenges 117
Tech for Mental Health 118
Tech for Social Skills and Emotional Regulation 119
Tech for Safety 120
How Much Tech is Too Much? 121

8. ⬢: INNER STRENGTH 123
Challenges Faced by Autistic Girls 125
Setting Healthy Boundaries 127
Goal-Setting Builds Resilience 131
Seeing Setbacks as Part of Growth 132
Showing Your Child the Value of Self-Compassion 134
Self-Acceptance and Radical Visibility 135
The Value of Positive Affirmations 137

9. **N: NAVIGATING STRESS AND ANXIETY AT SCHOOL**   141
    Anxiety in Autistic Girls   141
    How Can You Help Your Child?   145
    Battling Social Anxiety   146

10. **E: ENVISIONING THE FUTURE**   153
    Preparing Your Child for Her Transition to Middle School   154
    Preparing for Puberty   157
    Boosting Your Child's Independence   159
    Encouraging Self-Advocacy   163
    Preparing for Your Child's Academic Future   166
    Getting Your Child Excited About Future Career Options   166
    Estate Planning for Your Child   168

Conclusion   171
References   179

INTRODUCTION

> "Everyone has a mountain to climb, and Autism has not been my mountain; it has been my opportunity for victory."
>
> — RACHEL BARCELLONA (MAGRO, N.D.)

If you have already read my first book, *Raising an Autistic Girl: Modern ASD Strategies for Successful Parenting: Help Your Child Succeed in a Neurotypical World for a Life of Success on the Spectrum (5–11-year-olds)*, welcome back. If, on the other hand, this is your first time reading my work, I'd love to tell you a bit about myself. My name is Taylor Eberstadt, and I am a wife, a mom of two, and an author. I worked in the Army Reserves and as a teacher in Brisbane, Australia, where my wife and I live. I wrote my first book because childhood is a period I sometimes look back on with a mix of sadness and frustration. Sadness because I wasn't diagnosed with Autism until I was thirty and, therefore, never understood why it always seemed like I was different from everyone else. Frustration because back then, I thought I was supposed to be anyone else except me.

At school, I had many friends but felt that I had gained popularity by learning to "mask" my sensory challenges and other traits and quirks that were part of my authentic self. Autistic people know well what masking is. It's when we try our hardest to seem neurotypical, often at the expense of our well-being.

I never understood why it was so hard to understand irony or read others' nonverbal language, and I struggled to hold back my desire to stim when sensory overload took over. Texture mattered greatly to me … a soft carpet or velvet chair imbued a wonderful sense of tranquility, while scratchy clothing labels and tight clothing drove me crazy, as did the dreaded fruit cups they gave us at recess. Back then, exercise was my only solace … running until I dropped … until my mind was so tired that it stopped reliving events of the day and reminding me of things that made me feel like an outcast.

I also found classroom learning horrible because I needed more time than my classmates to process spoken words. When my teachers would explain something, they would go too fast for me to keep up. I would also get frustrated when they would move on to new topics or lessons because transitions have always been difficult for me. I had to develop my own way of notetaking, making small pictures next to complex topics, and spending extra hours at home learning the concepts taught in school. It was exhausting! To cope with it all, I would tense and release my calves. As a result, I developed amazing calf muscles.

Sensory difficulties and distraction were also major obstacles I faced daily. I would sit at the front of the class so I didn't have to "sift" through the varying objects, children, and classroom decorations in front. All these things made it harder for my mind to reach the teacher and the lessons she was trying to teach. I would go to the bathroom or get a drink from the water fountain if the class was becoming too loud during activities like model building in science. I'd also go to the library at break times because it was quiet. It made it even harder to maintain friendships when the library was my escape place!

My first book was written as a vindication of authenticity. It was a cry to parents worldwide to meet their children exactly where they are without unrealistic expectations or comparisons and without asking a child to be someone they are not. Even Autistic girls who seemingly "fit in" may still struggle at school or in their social lives, fearful of doing the things they need to calm down, scared of just being themselves. I advocated for the importance of letting children self-soothe the way they need to and encouraging them to dive deeply into their special interests—even if these lasted a few days, a week, or years.

I also stressed the importance of observing your child and understanding *their* way of communicating with you. While it is important to create a language-rich environment for your child and help them hone their communication skills, it is equally vital to be flexible and consider strategies such as learning American Sign Language (ASL) or Signing Exact English (SEE).

The theory of double empathy challenges the dominant idea that Autistic people need to be "cured" to fit in with others. There are proven brain differences that explain why Autistic people can have difficulty filtering sensory stimuli and language, and that means that many learning and communication tasks can be challenging for us. In *Raising an Autistic Girl*, I mentioned that when your daughter does not do what you ask, it is not because she wants to be difficult and frustrate you. It is just that her brain differences make it harder for her to do what may come so easily to those around her. My first book is a good place to start if your daughter has just been diagnosed with Autism. There are pros and cons to the choice of whether to obtain a diagnosis as well. There are many decisions to make, and it helps to have a comprehensive guide to accompany you throughout the process.

The book you have in your hands or on your screen right now is a different story. This book is all about one of the most important and longest stages in your daughter's life: her school years. For me, they were some of the most challenging of my life. My parents made an effort to send me to a good school, but I struggled to find unconditional friends and was a victim of bullying and sexual assault. As soon as I published my first book, I knew that my next work would *have* to be about helping Autistic girls during their school years.

I love frameworks, as they serve as reminders of what I am reading or studying. For this book, I have chosen the acronym G.I.R.L.S. S.H.I.N.E. Each of these letters stands for a different chapter in the book and represents a specific component of school life. The book is divided into ten chapters as follows:

- **Growing Through Challenges at School:** Teaching a child how to deal with sensory, academic, and social challenges at school and beyond
- **Investigating School Options:** How to decide between different school types and educational plans
- **Routines that Foster Success:** Morning, afternoon, and evening routines to help an Autistic girl learn, play, and rest
- **Learning Strategies for Academic Growth:** Vital strategies that can boost an Autistic girl's academic progress
- **Sensory Success:** How Autistic girls can deal with sensory challenges and changes to routines when they arise
- **Seeking Connection:** Building a rich social life and finding a child's "strawberry people"
- **Harnessing Smart Technology:** Top tech and apps for learning, socialization, and more
- **Inner Strength:** How to cultivate an Autistic child's resilience against bullying and other negative behaviors they may encounter at school
- **Navigating Anxiety and Stress at School:** Strategies to deal with social anxiety and stress
- **Envisioning the Future:** How to help a child set goals and transition to Middle School

This book is an exhaustive guide to navigating the main challenges of school life for Autistic girls in the areas of learning, sensory stimuli, and social interaction. We will also delve into tougher issues, such as how to help your child deal with stress and anxiety, boost her resilience to bullying, and prevent and report any instances of assault. I will once again advocate for supporting your child fully, accepting and celebrating her authenticity every step of the way.

This book will focus on harnessing practical strategies to help you work alongside teachers, boost your daughter's self-esteem and confidence, and encourage her to follow her passions. It will highlight the importance of surrounding her with people who love and accept her unconditionally.

This book is peppered with real-life testimonies from parents, students, and members of the Autistic community. I will also be sharing my own stories, something I find incredibly liberating after spending much of my childhood trying to hide who I was, fearful of others' judgment, shame, and criticism. You are your child's parent, best friend, and fiercest advocate. That is why it is important to know the precise challenges you will encounter, as well as your child's strengths, her allies, and the therapists and professionals who can help her live her fullest life. I will accompany you every step of the way, starting with the first chapter, which will center on the main challenges Autistic girls face at school.

G: GROWING THROUGH CHALLENGES AT SCHOOL

"Autism is not a tragedy. Ignorance is the tragedy."

— KERRY MAGRO

I went to an all-girls school in Brisbane, Australia, and wish I could say that I had more positive memories. I admit it's hard to listen to adult friends who went to similar schools and say they formed the backdrop to some of the best memories of their childhood. My experience was marked by social hierarchy, social exclusion, and many more psychological games. I had a group of friends but didn't feel particularly connected to any of them. Being accepted in that group meant having to mask 24/7. I used to have little scripts I would learn so I could say the right thing. Often, I didn't know if they were saying something seriously or in jest, whether they truly saw me as "one of them" or were merely humoring me. I had difficulty identifying irony and sometimes made the mistake of laughing at the wrong time, incurring their annoyance or anger.

My schoolmates used to call me an oddball, but I was (to some extent) "accepted" because I adhered to their conventions and pretended to like the things they did. Having a group of friends also shielded me from the school's biggest bullies. As I shared earlier, I was a victim of sexual assault more than once, and I knew that if I were alone, I would be far more vulnerable. After school, I could not wait to get into the shower and "wash off" the exhaustion from having to constantly hide my deep desire to stim, talk about my interests, or run away. If you read my first book, then you know that sport (particularly running) has always been my salvation. It was the one way I could avoid thinking about the shame and discomfort I had to face daily. Today, social interactions with other moms at my children's school still overwhelm me. I put on a brave face but calmed my frazzled nerves by going for a drive and drowning my stress in loud music. I have always loved the freedom that taking the wheel bestows.

Of course, back then, I had not been diagnosed yet, so the reason why I struggled so much was a mystery to me. I wished desperately to be homeschooled, but that option was not available to me. In a way, I felt that homeschooling would have suited me more and allowed me to focus more on my studies. I would have been more comfortable and confident, and I undoubtedly would have been in a better state of mind to concentrate. Once I was diagnosed and Autism itself became a special interest to devote years of study to, I realized that my social and other challenges were shared by so many Autistic girls and women I subsequently met. In this chapter, I'd like to focus on what Autism is and how it can impact girls' learning journeys. I hope that the testimonies of other girls and women I share throughout this book help you grasp the extent to which you are most certainly not alone.

WHAT IS AUTISM AND HOW DOES IT IMPACT GIRLS?

Autism spectrum disorder (ASD) comprises a broad range of conditions that can manifest themselves in difficulties with social skills, repetitive behaviors, and speech and nonverbal communication. It currently affects one in thirty-six children and one in forty-five adults in the US (Autism Speaks, n.d.-a). Autistic girls and boys often have difficulties at school because of the following challenges (National Autistic Society, n.d.-a):

- **Social Communication and Social Interaction Challenges:** Autistic people have difficulties interpreting verbal and nonverbal language, including gestures and tone of voice. Some have limited speech or are completely nonverbal, while others have excellent language skills but may struggle to understand irony and other nuances in language. For instance, they may need more time to process information. They may also take things literally and find it hard to understand abstract concepts.

  Some Autistic people repeat whole chunks of what they read or hear (echolalia) in unrelated contexts. They may also find it hard to understand others' emotions and express their own. They may appear insensitive, prefer to spend time alone, or behave in a way others deem "strange." As a result, being with other kids for so many hours at school can be incredibly draining to them.

- **Repetitive Behavior:** When Autistic people feel overwhelmed by sensory stimuli such as lights and noise, they may aim to soothe themselves through repetitive movements such as rocking, hand-flapping, twirling, and similar behaviors. They may get very distressed when changes to routine occur and prefer to eat the same foods and wear the same items of clothing.
- **Sensory Differences:** Autistic people may be over- or under-sensitive to sensory input such as smells, tastes, light, colors, temperature, sounds, or pain. For instance, when classmates are noisy, it may cause a child anxiety or even pain. They may not enjoy being hugged, which can lead others to mislabel them as aloof.

- **Extreme Anxiety, Meltdowns, and Shutdowns:** Change and sensory stimuli may be so distressing to us that we may struggle against anxiety and emotional regulation. Over one-third of Autistic people have mental health issues. When we are overwhelmed in a situation, we may have a meltdown (cry, shout, or lash out) or, on the contrary, completely shut down. It may suddenly seem as though we have "switched off."

> *"When I was at school, I found it hard to talk to most people, including most of my teachers. Even those I could relate to more were sometimes hard to communicate with because I always felt anxious about speaking my mind. One day, I had anxiety and stayed outside the classroom, trying to soothe myself by breathing like my mom had taught me to do. When my teacher saw I was outside, she told me, "Get back in class right now," and my anxiety got worse, and I had a panic attack. She kept repeating, "Tell me what is bothering you so I can help you." I froze on the spot. I was hyperventilating and felt like I couldn't speak a word or move an inch. She kept telling me to sit down, and finally, I managed to shuffle into the classroom and fall into my seat. All I wanted to do was run out of there, but I felt too weak to walk. My teacher kept saying things like, "There's no reason to get this upset," and I felt so judged at that moment. While I was still crying and hyperventilating, she told me to study for the test she was about to give. I had forgotten that we had a test and had not revised. This made me start shaking, and tears began falling from my eyes. I think I answered one or two questions out of fifty because I was so upset. When I got home, my mother was upset, too, because she could see my eyes were swollen, and I had been crying. She could not understand why the teacher hadn't tried to do more to help me when I was in a state of panic."*
>
> — MARIANNE, 23

DIFFERENCES IN THE AUTISTIC BRAIN

In my first book, I delved deeply into the major brain differences between Autistic and neurotypical brains. Neuroimaging studies have revealed that Autistic individuals have differences throughout the cerebral cortex—the part of the brain containing billions of neurons involved in high-level executive functions such as understanding complex or abstract concepts, solving problems, and managing relationships. Changes have also been observed in the anterior cingulate cortex, which is involved in decision-making, impulse control, emotional regulation, and attention. Another study found differences in eleven cortical regions, including those involved in language, mental flexibility, reasoning, and cognition (UCLA Health 2022).

Studies have shown that in Autistic people, VENS neurons, which are used to process complex situations rapidly and intuitively, display delayed and reduced development (Guo et al. 2019). In my first book, I delved into one of the leading theories that explain why Autistic people face the specific challenges they do. This theory embraces a model of "cortical hyperexcitability" (Takarae and Sweeney 2017). It espouses that our brain gets excited easily, and we can't tell the difference between what we want to ignore and what we need to pay attention to.

Two more recent studies have revealed vital insights about Autistic brain differences. One showed that the Autistic brain has differences in the "white matter tract" microstructure in the brain stem. These differences are related to sensory responses, and they are extremely reflective or difficult to control (Rivera-Bonet 2023). The second study found that two specific nuclei in the brain stem contribute to gastrointestinal issues and trouble with eating and swallowing—issues that are common in the Autistic community (Leclerc 2024).

I have presented these findings briefly here because they reveal that so many of the behaviors that may be frustrating for both children and parents—for instance, difficulties with following instructions or paying attention—are simply beyond a child's control. Expecting an Autistic child to behave like a neurotypical one is not only futile but often harmful to their self-confidence and outlook. In contrast, unconditional acceptance and focusing on a child's strengths and interests are far more positive and fruitful strategies to adopt when you are helping a child deal with the social, sensory, and learning challenges they may face at school.

AUTISM IN GIRLS

Another factor that can affect a girl's experience at school is the lack of awareness of how Autism manifests in girls and boys. The Diagnostic and Statistical Manual of Mental Disorders, 5th edition, text revision (DSM-5-TR) does not differentiate between the symptoms of ASD in boys and girls, focusing instead on behaviors that can be common to both—including struggles with social interaction, nonverbal communication, and unpredictable situations. However, there are key differences in how Autism manifests itself in girls and boys. For instance, during the elementary school years, girls can be very chatty and may form large groups, while boys may prefer playing alone (Attwood 2007). This is because girls can be more efficient at "masking" their Autism than boys.

In the book *Unmasking Autism*, writer Devon Price divides the traits expressed by Autistic girls into four categories: emotional, psychological, behavioral, and social (Price 2022). For instance, in the emotional sphere, they may seem more immature than their neurotypical peers and have meltdowns or cry about matters that seem insignificant to others. At times, they may notice that someone is upset but not be sure how to support them. This can lead them to doubt their abilities to form connections. Because they can be highly efficient at masking, they may lack energy after interacting with others socially.

Psychologically, Autistic girls may have higher rates of depression, anxiety, and social anxiety than others (Yau et al. 2023). They may have a big need to be accepted and a deep insecurity about their likability. They also have specific behavioral tendencies, including working out intensely and counting calories. Furthermore, they may be very strict with themselves and their environment to reduce the stress associated with the unknown and seem more logical than neurotypical girls. Some may have specific sensory preferences when it comes to food and textures, displaying a big aversion to one or more types of food.

Finally, in the social sense, they may fit in very well in groups but have just one or two close friends or an imaginary friend. They may be generally quiet but speak profusely about a topic they are interested in. Some Autistic girls may seem very extroverted when approached but avoid starting conversations. Some may not enjoy sharing and either insist that games be played according to their rules or go along with the leaders of their group. They often have a deep-seated fear of disappointing others or being judged (Attwood 2007).

HOW DOES AUTISM AFFECT GIRLS' LEARNING?

All the differences I presented above explain why an Autistic girl's learning experiences can be stressful. Neurotypical children may struggle to focus in class or resist the impulse to talk with their classmates while the teacher is talking. However, a child with Autism may face all these challenges and find it difficult to work out what their teacher is asking them to do. They may not understand the sequence of steps they need to complete an exercise or test. They may dread recess because it once again means having to make their way through a labyrinth of gestures, nuances, and people saying one thing but meaning another. Some girls may wonder if they are really accepted or merely tolerated, not to mention all the sensory challenges they may have to face, including foods with textures that upset them or lights and noises that can make it impossible to focus on what their teachers or friends are saying. Their teacher won't necessarily know all the problems they are facing. They may think that your daughter is simply being willful or stubborn. In fact, she may desperately want to fulfill others' expectations and follow instructions but have numerous obstacles firing at her all at once.

Just a few specific challenges your child may face in the realm of learning include:

- **Executive Function Challenges:** Executive functioning refers to the ability to process information. It includes skills like organizing, planning, paying attention, and inhibiting inappropriate responses (Autism Speaks, n.d.-b). Children with difficulties in this area may find it hard to stay organized, follow a sequence of information, or regulate their emotions. As such, they may answer a teacher or classmate inappropriately, find it hard to concentrate on classwork, or be unable to control their impulses. They may also struggle to make connections between concepts or ideas. Some girls may learn better through images than through words.
- **Verbal and Language Skills:** Autistic people have a wide range of communication abilities. Some are chatty and extroverted, while others may find some or all areas of communication challenging. Those who do not communicate verbally may use behaviors to communicate how they are feeling. For instance, they may have a meltdown or refuse to follow instructions because they don't know how to communicate that they are tired, unhappy, or scared (Autism Awareness Australia, n.d.-a).

    As mentioned above, they may use learned phrases (echolalia) obtained from friends, family, a YouTube video, or a film. They may use these phrases to ask for something they want, start a game related to the phrase, draw attention to something, or self-soothe. That is, an echolalic phrase may seem unrelated to the context, but it may make full sense once you observe why your child is using it.

Some Autistic people may repeat a question someone has posed to indicate they agree with what has been said. Their language may be literal and matter-of-fact, and they may deliver their messages with a seemingly inexpressive tone of voice. They may also change their accents when talking.

In chapter 10, I will share the benefits of working alongside both sensory and speech therapists to help your child develop verbal language skills and understand language through pictures.

- **Sensory Processing Issues:** A child who is struggling to process sensory input may seem inattentive, distracted, distressed, or anxious. This may lead to limited participation in the classroom or meltdowns and shutdowns when sensory input becomes too overwhelming (NHS Essex Partnership University, n.d.).
- **Alexithymia:** Around 49.93 percent of people with Autism have alexithymia, a condition in which one has challenges identifying and describing one's feelings and distinguishing between feelings and bodily sensations (Embrace Autism 2024). Both Autistic traits and alexithymia decrease prosocial interaction (the enjoyment of having kind, reciprocal relationships), but alexithymia does so more severely. Both also decrease sociability, which can affect a child's relationships with others at school and beyond.

"I am a teacher of primary school students and enjoy bringing my experiences and insight to both my neurotypical and ASD students. One thing I find very useful is to use visual cues like pictures and comics to illustrate points for my students with ASD. As a child, I understood images much more than words, and I still enjoy learning with infographics, photographs, and sketches more than books. I notice that images, maps, and photographs help my students memorize information."

— LILIANE, 38

AUTISM AND LEARNING DISORDERS

Learning disorders alter brain functioning in a way that affects the cognitive processes related to learning. Autism is linked to some disorders, including dyslexia, which impacts the ability to read, owing to challenges in word recognition and decoding (Goldstar Rehabilitation 2023). Other learning disabilities that may affect children with Autism include dyscalculia (difficulty with mathematical concepts, leading to challenges in understanding numbers and performing calculations) and dysgraphia (difficulties with spelling, writing, and organizing one's thoughts on paper) (Allstar ABA Therapy, n.d.).

AUTISM AND ADHD

Attention-deficit/hyperactivity disorder, or ADHD, is not a learning disorder, but it can interact with learning disorders and add obstacles to a child's learning journey. Studies have shown that as many as 30 to 50 percent of children with ASD also have symptoms of ADHD, including hyperactivity, sensory processing issues, and difficulty sustaining attention and concentration. Like Autism, ADHD influences executive function, making time management, planning, and sustained focus more difficult to achieve (Gehret 2020a).

HOW LEARNING DISORDERS CAN AFFECT A CHILD'S MENTAL HEALTH

Learning difficulties, coupled with Autism, can lead to mental health conditions such as anxiety, with statistics showing that as many as one in five adults with ASD have this disorder. Autism also carries a higher risk of depression and other mental disorders. Many Autism-related health conditions stem from numerous causes, both genetic and environmental. For instance, not having access to treatment and resources can increase stress and lead to conditions that worsen without treatment. Moreover, the issues I have mentioned above—social difficulties, sensory issues, communication challenges, bullying, and stigma can all trigger anxiety and depression. It is vital to be on the lookout for symptoms of depression and anxiety and to create a positive environment for your child and help them make healthy lifestyle choices (Gehret 2020b).

AUTISM AND SELF-ESTEEM

Autism can also impact your daughter's self-esteem. One study (van der Cruijsen and Boyer 2020) showed that young people with Autism report lower levels of this quality than neurotypical youths. Self-esteem issues can be caused by the many differences that exist between Autistic people and their neurotypical peers (including motor difficulties, language issues, or differing intellectual abilities that can impact academic achievement). Low self-esteem is a risk factor for developing depressive, anxious, uncooperative, or aggressive symptoms, and it needs to be taken seriously.

In my experience and that of many of my peers and friends, one of the most powerful ways to boost a child's self-esteem and self-confidence is to provide them with numerous opportunities to immerse themselves in the activities they enjoy. Give your child praise for completing tasks and being so engaged in what she does. Use positive reinforcement to highlight positive behaviors such as sharing with others or asking for something she needs. Interacting with others can help a child grow more confident in their abilities, so acknowledging all their efforts at communication can encourage them to further develop their social skills (The Spectrum, n.d.).

LEARNED HELPLESSNESS AND TASK AVOIDANCE

Learned helplessness, task avoidance, and procrastination can also affect the self-esteem of children with ASD and ADHD. Successfully completing tasks designed for neurotypical children to neurotypical standards can be tough on an Autistic brain. That means that all too often, Autistic children are told that they are doing things "wrong." They may constantly be told they need to make more eye contact, follow instructions more attentively, stop moving in their seats, or organize themselves better. All these messages can chip away at their self-confidence, leading them to feel powerless and incompetent. The result is learned helplessness—a protective mechanism that leads them to procrastinate to avoid having to face failure (Long 2024). It may seem like the Autistic person is being lazy, but their behavior is actually based on a deep fear that they won't be successful at what they set out to do.

To battle learned helplessness, start by being aware of the sometimes unrealistic expectations placed on neurodivergent people to conform to neurotypical standards. Remind your child that many people struggle to adhere to these standards and that not meeting them does not make people defective or lesser. Help her find support systems or accommodations that can make it easier for her to perform the tasks she wishes to complete. Encourage her to share her preferences, styles, and habits with others so that others can understand that her approach may be different, it is not inferior. Teach her how to set short, achievable goals and how to break them down into individual steps. Celebrate each step she completes. Say she has to write a paragraph about a book. You can consider breaking this task up into the following steps:

- Ask your child to answer these questions about the book:
  - What is it about?
  - Who are the main characters?
  - What happens to them?
- Help her pick one idea to write about. For example, your child may wish to write about the characters going on an adventure.
- Write three sentences about that idea. For instance:
  - Max and Lena enter a magical forest.
  - They meet strange creatures who teach them how to be brave.
  - Max and Lena return home feeling more powerful and confident.

When helping your child set goals, try to make them as relevant as possible to her areas of interest. The more relevant the goal is, the more likely she is to get straight to the task and complete it. It can also be very helpful to teach her about thought distortions like "permanence," "pervasiveness," and "personalization" (Moore 2023), three concepts that merit definition.

- **Permanence:** A distortion that leads some people to believe that if they fail at something one time, they will always do badly at it. If you notice your child feels this way, give her specific examples that show this isn't true. For instance, if she is having difficulty drawing something, you can talk about the many beautiful drawings she has completed in the past.
- **Pervasiveness:** The idea that if you have difficulties in one area, you will have difficulties with *everything* in life. Once again, you can help your child evade this way of thinking by pointing out her specific strengths and providing examples of how she has employed them in the past.
- **Personalization:** Assuming that when we are successful, it's just "good luck," but when something bad happens, it is "our fault." Teach your child to notice the negative messages she

sends herself and to reframe them into more positive thoughts. For instance, if she says something like, "My friend was upset today because I didn't talk to them enough," you can help her depersonalize this event by showing her how to send herself a more positive message, such as, "My friend might be upset because of something else going on in their life, and it's not my fault."

Finally, encourage your child to be independent. Specialist Dr. Debra Moore recalls how a lovely story that successful author Temple Grandin told her. When Temple was a child, she was building something and needed a piece of wood to complete it. She was scared of going to the store herself, but her mother, knowing of her daughter's strong special interest in making things, was sure she could manage just fine. Temple explained, "She refused to go with me because she figured my motivation to finish the project would override my anxiety and reluctance. She was right. I went to the store, got the wood, finished the design, and felt proud of myself" (Moore 2023). Her story shows that one of the best ways to empower your child is to give her a great reason to face her fears and realize how capable she is.

THE IMPORTANCE OF RECEIVING AN EARLY DIAGNOSIS

If you read my first book, then you know I believe in the power of early diagnosis. It was such a relief to me to know that there was an explanation behind so many of the things I struggled with—the meaningless small talk with others, having to learn what was appropriate or not to say, feeling like I lacked empathy, and getting angry at myself for only wanting to talk about what interested me. Having said that, I know people who disagree.

Some parents feel that obtaining a diagnosis will result in their child being stigmatized. Certainly, there is a great lack of understanding about Autism and its signs, which can lead to painful stereotypes and misunderstandings. Stigmatization can adversely affect a child's physical and mental health and their social connections. Parents, families, loved ones, and friends need to work to reduce Autism stigma. We can do this by reading, sharing key information, and promoting positive portrayals of people with Autism in the media.

Some parents prefer not to pursue a formal diagnosis because they believe their child can progress better without a label. Moreover, they wish to avoid triggering emotions like frustration or sadness, which can arise when a definitive diagnosis cannot be made.

I can only speak of my experience, and how relieving it was to receive my diagnosis as a thirtieth birthday present to myself. It's logical to worry about a child being labeled, but I also feel that there are many advantages to having a formal diagnosis. One of these is the chance to access specialized services and therapies, such as speech therapy and occupational therapy. These tools can help a child advance in leaps and bounds in terms of communication, social interaction, and learning. A diagnosis can also help you seek an Individualized Education Program (IEP) for your child, which can ensure she receives the help she needs in class and provide her with useful accommodations at school.

When you know your child has Autism, you can actively seek out a supportive community of fellow parents, therapists, and friends who have encountered the challenges you are going through. They can recommend great professionals and reading material, provide support when you're feeling overwhelmed, and provide inspiration for your family's journey. This connection is beneficial for your child as well since it can open doors to friendships with other Autistic children (Abrams, n.d.). As I mentioned in my first book, research has shown that Autistic people often find relationships with other Autistic people less stressful and tiring and more fulfilling in terms of communication and understanding (Crompton et al. 2020).

"I was very relieved when I was diagnosed with Autism a year ago. I knew something was different about me, and everyone always called me dramatic, stupid, or stubborn. My mom told me she read somewhere that 'it can be comforting to know you are a zebra instead of a strange horse.' Now I know what brings other zebras happiness, and I can hang out with them. My fellow zebras make me feel I am a beautiful zebra instead of a failed horse."

— JUNO, 14

End-of-Chapter Activity: Journal Reflections

In chapter 2, we will discuss different school options you may consider for your child. Before you continue reading, however, I suggest that you take your journal and write down your answers to the following questions.

1. What do I anticipate will be some of my child's biggest challenges at school?
2. What strengths or interests does my child have that could help her enjoy school more?
3. Are there any sensory sensitivities my child has that might affect her comfort at school?
4. How do I envision success for my child in the school environment, and how can I help her achieve it?
5. What tools or accommodations might help my child thrive in her academic and social activities?
6. How can I communicate openly with my child to better understand her feelings about school?
7. How can I work with teachers and school staff to create a supportive learning environment and ensure teachers are on my child's side?

I hope that as you progress through this book, you will have many more questions and answers that you can use when you deal with teachers, parents, and other significant people in your child's life!

1: INVESTIGATING SCHOOL OPTIONS

> *"It's really cool that everybody's a little bit different, but the same, too."*
>
> — JULIA FROM SESAME STREET. (TWINKLE, N.D.)

I mentioned earlier that if I had been able to choose which type of school to attend, my option would have been homeschooling. All school options have pros and cons. However, because I am a reflective learner, I used to find it very stressful when the teacher would move from topic to topic at a faster pace than I could keep up with. I had many strategies to help me concentrate and learn (such as drawing pictures while note-taking), but I never had time to use them in class.

At home, I employed many self-soothing strategies to stay focused. For instance, I used to hum while reading long texts and use a chair massager to keep myself seated. I also used to rub my feet over a pressure point foot massager and eat crunchy snacks while studying. None of these (except the crunchy snacks) were available to me during the hours I spent at school. I felt like I had run a marathon by the time I got home, except the day was far from done. I had to redo all my notes, which took hours, and that was time I could have devoted to the things I loved. Of course, my story may be very different from your child's, and that is why finding the right school is a personal journey. In this chapter, I will present a few considerations and options to help you select a school with the accommodations your child needs.

SCHOOL OPTIONS

The Individuals with Disabilities Education Act (IDEA) obliges school districts to provide the "least restrictive environment" for a child's education. That means that districts must consider options such as inclusion in classrooms before placing a child in a more specialized setting. If you prefer your child to be in a specialized setting, you may need to demonstrate that the inclusion strategies adopted are not working before the district funds tuition for a specialized school.

Autistic children typically qualify for an Individualized Education Program (IEP) or a 504 Plan, both of which I will discuss in this chapter. However, just because they have a diagnosis of Autism does not mean they automatically qualify for accommodations. Instead, the district's child study team determines whether they need additional support (Rudy 2024a).

Inclusion

Inclusion describes a situation in which a child is in a typical classroom environment but has a few accommodations set up for them. The child is expected to self-regulate in large groups, follow the teacher's directions, and work at (or close to) the expected grade level. This setting works best for kids who are as independent (or more so) than their classmates and those without big social challenges. This setting may be particularly tough for an Autistic girl who is nonverbal or one who has anxiety or meltdowns owing to sensory challenges. The upside of this option is that a child follows a standard education program alongside their peers. The downside is that it may lead them to adopt masking behaviors, which can interfere with their learning and self-esteem and potentially cause problems like anxiety and depression (Autistic Girls at School, n.d.).

Inclusion with an Individualized Education Program (IEP) or 504 Plan

This option describes a typical classroom environment where a child has a personalized program (an IEP or 504 Plan) to help them achieve their learning goals. Let's briefly discuss the differences between the two:

- **Individualized Education Program/IEP:** An IEP falls under the Individuals with Disabilities Act (IDEA). It provides special education services to elementary or secondary students with an identified disability that impacts their academic progress. Before special education services are provided to your child, it may be necessary to obtain further assessments after your child is diagnosed with Autism. These may include an unstructured diagnostic play session, developmental evaluation, speech-language assessment, evaluation of behavior and adaptive or real-life skills, and a parent interview. These evaluations provide much more comprehensive information about your child and their strengths and needs, which are helpful in creating a personalized plan.

  An IEP is developed by the child, their family or designated advocates, and a team of individuals from various academic disciplines. It usually includes (Access Computing, n.d.):

    - The child's progress in the general curriculum
    - All services the child qualifies for
    - Accommodations the child requires to thrive, such as classroom accommodations

- The child's present level of educational performance
- Measurable annual goals and objectives for the child's education
- Modifications to the curriculum required by the child, plus therapies such as speech, occupational, and physical therapy

When attending an IEP meeting, know that your child has a right to assistive technology to improve critical skills if your IEP team believes that this technology will benefit your child's education (Autism Speaks, n.d.-c). If the IEP team is unable to determine which assistive devices best suit your child's needs, then a formal assistive technology evaluation will need to be carried out.

- **504 Plan:** A 504 Plan falls within the scope of the Rehabilitation Act of 1973. It spells out accommodations for students with a physical or emotional disability. It allows for special accommodations such as extra breaks, fidgets, modified homework, and extra time for taking tests and completing assignments. The rules for the creation of a 504 Plan are less restrictive than those for IEPs. The team that creates this plan may include the child's parent or caregiver, general and special education teachers, and/or the school principal (Rawe 2024).

Although there are many specific differences between the two plans, an IEP is considered a more comprehensive and tailored approach to supporting a child with Autism. With an IEP, your child may enjoy one-on-one support, counseling, or specialized interventions, depending on her needs. For children who do well academically but may require certain accommodations or modifications to their learning environment to thrive, a 504 may be enough.

If you opt for inclusion and an educational program or plan, your child may benefit from having a 1:1 aide. This person can help her with various goals, including behavior management, instructional support, daily living activities (such as toileting), social skills, safety, and more. Before your child can obtain 1:1 support, your district will likely conduct an assessment to determine whether she qualifies for it (Undivided 2024).

Many parents choose inclusion with the support of an IEP or 504 Plan because they see it as a middle ground between inclusion and special education. It can be a good option for independent kids who can regulate their emotions. However, kids in typical classrooms may be more likely to experience bullying and put-downs. What's more, not all 1:1 aides are specifically trained to work with kids with Autism, and there is no guarantee your child will be granted an aide. If you think your child will benefit from an aide, identify the specific skills she needs help with (for instance, speech development). Try to compile and submit as much data as possible, indicating that she requires additional support to progress. Finally, always let your daughter lead the way when it comes to aides. She may not necessarily gel with her aide, and this may pose an additional challenge to her learning journey. If you suspect this is the case, speak to your IEP team about what is going on, compiling data that shows that your daughter may benefit from having a different aide assigned to her.

Special Education

Under the special education model, kids attend class in a special education classroom in their local public school. The pros of this type of setting are that classes are usually smaller, children are included in all activities and events, and there is ample opportunity to work on social skills. Special education is often the chosen option when kids struggle with academics. For Autistic kids who are progressing academically but need help with social skills, it may not be the best option.

Autistic Support Classrooms

Some public schools in larger school districts have Autistic support classrooms, which are specifically created to meet the needs of Autistic kids and staffed by teachers and aides who have been trained in Autism and education. They have several advantages, including a higher adult-to-child ratio and specialized teaching tools, and they often focus on areas like social skills and speech. Their pros include the fact that children get to spend most of their day with other Autistic children, which means they don't have to mask and can self-soothe as they need to. On the downside, they may feel segregated from other students in their school.

Moreover, classes may focus on skills your child does not have difficulties with (for instance, social skills) and neglect the child's academic abilities and interests. Finally, some Autistic support classrooms utilize applied behavioral therapy (ABA) techniques. As mentioned in my previous book, ABA is considered effective for some kids, but it is controversial because it involves training Autistic kids to behave like neurotypical children. As stated by Autistic self-advocate Ari Ne'eman, "The emphasis on things like eye contact or sitting still or not stimming is oriented around trying to create the trappings of the typical child, without acknowledging the reality that different children have different needs. It can be actively harmful when we teach people from a very early age that the way they act, the way they move is fundamentally wrong" (Garey, n.d.).

Private Schools

If your child excels academically and is happy to socialize with neurotypical people, private schooling may be a good choice. It has specific advantages such as smaller classes and good resources. However, most schools of this type don't make accommodations for Autism. Some big cities have private schools specifically for children with learning disabilities or behavioral problems, and some have schools that specialize exclusively in Autism. They may be a good match for your child if she struggles in neurotypical settings and is unhappy with other options you have tried.

The upside is being able to deal with staff members who are knowledgeable about Autism and can offer numerous resources, ranging from sensory classrooms to quiet nooks for calming down. These schools typically have occupational and behavioral therapists on staff, which is a bonus. Equally positive is the self-confidence boost your child can receive from interacting with other Autistic kids, without the need to mask and without the inevitable bullying and/or teasing that takes place in neurotypical schools.

If you're interested in a school such as this, find out more about what type of approaches they offer. Some utilize ABA therapy, so ask about that during the research stage. The downside of private education is its cost. If your earnings are standing in the way of private schooling, consider hiring a lawyer or specialized advocate to convince the district to pay for your child's education.

Specialized Charter Schools

Charter schools are public schools run by private organizations or groups. Some focus on the arts or sciences, while others are designed for children with ASD, such as the South Florida Autism Charter Schools, which provide educational and therapeutic services to children with ASD living in specific counties. These schools are free to attend, but students must apply to be admitted and meet eligibility requirements. Their benefits include specialized staff who are trained to teach kids with Autism. The downside is the fact that there may not be schools such as this in your area, and even if they do exist, your child may not meet their eligibility requirements (Leventhal 2024).

Homeschooling and Online Schooling

The obvious benefits of homeschooling include being able to advance at a child's chosen pace, the ability to follow preset routines, and the elimination of distractions and sensory obstacles to learning. The main obstacle in homeschooling is time. If you have a full-time job, for instance, you may not have enough time to offer your child a truly enriching homeschooling experience. It is also important to consider whether your child will be able to re-enter the school system and take public exams if she wishes to do so in the future. Parents of home-schooled kids need to take the time to create numerous social opportunities for their kids. This can be achieved by joining support groups and signing your daughter up for numerous activities in her areas of interest.

Another option is online schooling. Currently, there are numerous online learning options for kids in elementary, middle, and high school. These include online classes, online schools with live teaching, and self-paced online schools, which allow kids to work through digital modules at their own pace. Some online learning options are accredited (for instance, self-paced online schools), while others (such as those following an online curriculum with interactive digital lessons) are not. Some mix digital content with live teaching.

Unschooling

Unschooling is a pedagogical approach that allows a child's natural curiosity and energy to direct their learning. Unschoolers do not follow a formal curriculum. Nor do they take tests or receive grades. Parents act as facilitators for their kids, exposing them to a myriad of interesting topics and trusting their children to learn as naturally as they would learn any other skill. It can work well for kids with special interests who enjoy having the time to immerse themselves in deep knowledge about their chosen topic.

Writer Ann Gaydos, who is a mom to an Autistic girl, recalls how well this school worked for her daughter and her second child. Gaydos states that when people insisted that Autistic children benefited from structured classes, she would answer, "My children were both safe and learning and that I could hardly do worse for my Autistic child than her public school … had done. Her education was proceeding forward rather than (as at school) in the reverse direction. Nobody was injuring or isolating her in seclusion for hours at a stretch. Nobody was putting her life at risk …" Today, Gaydos's older daughter is a volunteer with Alliance Against Seclusion and Restraint, which was formed to raise awareness about the use of aversive discipline practices (Gaydos 2023).

Factors to Consider When Making a Choice

When choosing between different schooling options, there are many factors to consider, including:

- Your child's academic skills
- How she interacts with kids in large groups
- The training teachers and staff have in your shortlist of schools
- What activities and therapies are offered in different schools
- The extent to which schools can accommodate your child's different needs, including sensory and learning needs
- How schools deal with communication of progress reports, how often they are willing to meet with you, and what communication style they encourage
- How your child feels about different options and the type of setting she feels most comfortable with
- The extent to which your child can focus in class
- Your child's communication abilities and level of social engagement
- Previous experiences your child may have had in class

- Whether medical staff is available in case of medical emergencies

The more you research, ask other parents, read books and blog posts, and contact local schools, the more confident you can feel about making the best choice for your child's abilities, wants, and needs.

> "I was homeschooled from the age of six because I had many meltdowns at school because of sensory problems. At home, my mom has created a space where I can learn about robotics and take equipment apart and put it back together. The room is quiet and has lots of plants, and I feel so at peace there. I feel like I am getting to know so much more about robots than I could at school. I enjoy studying math and science and can share so many facts about forests from all over the world. I am happy because my dad and mom take me to museums, parks, and other places where I can learn about the world. They signed me up for robotics classes close to where my school used to be, and I love meeting other kids who enjoy my hobby."
>
> — MAX, 13

> "I have two Autistic daughters—Maxine, aged eight, and Evan, aged five. Initially, my husband and I sent Evan to school because we felt she would benefit from a more structured approach. However, after a couple of terms, she asked if she could be homeschooled like Maxine. We mostly opt for the natural learning/unschooling approach, allowing our daughters' interests to lead the way. We are thinking of finding an online school because I feel a bit burned out from taking care of our home and both of them, and I am thinking of going back to work part-time. I love guiding them in their studies and am especially happy I can take them to places and take

part in activities that allow them to advance in their areas of interest."

— LUZ, 42

"*My younger daughter Amina has been attending an online school for a year. The school is very flexible, and they look for ways to make sure she has everything she needs to succeed. Amina has ADHD, so it is sometimes hard for her to get her work done on time, but the school is very understanding and never makes her feel like a failure when she struggles with deadlines. They offer her one-on-one tutoring and remove assignments if Amina has already shown that she knows the topic well but cannot complete an assignment because of her struggles.*"

— HAROUN, 48

EXTENDED SCHOOL YEAR (ESY) SERVICES

The end of the school year or breaks, such as winter or spring break, can be a difficult transition for Autistic girls and boys, as it may block the progress they have been making. If this is the case for your daughter, check to see if she is eligible for Extended School Year (ESY) services over the summer break. These services are defined in the IDEA, though eligibility depends on a decision made by the child's IEP team. The most important consideration is whether the child is at risk of losing vital skills and knowledge during a long break from school and how long it will take to regain these skills. If the team believes that a long break will significantly delay a child's progress when they return from school, they will determine the best plan to ensure this doesn't happen. They will also make an effort to match ESY services to the specific skills your child is working on, such as speech, language, or other skills. ESY services vary greatly. Sometimes, they are provided in person, while at others, they are provided in the form of instructions for home-based activities you can help your child with. In cases where a higher level of support is required, ESY services may be offered to your child full time (Autism Speaks, n.d.-d).

TIPS FOR WORKING WITH TEACHERS

If you opt for schooling outside your home, your child's teachers can be your best allies, so it is vital to build a good relationship with them from the very start. Your child's teacher will need to know key information that only you can give them, including your child's sensory challenges. In Chapter 5, we will delve more deeply into how to discuss sensory challenges with teachers, though the information you find there should ideally be brought up as early as your first meeting with your child's school and teachers.

Once you pick a school, I recommend taking steps to identify key staff members in the school who can help create an optimal learning environment for your child. Make contact with them early and set a positive, friendly, open tone so that teachers know they can discuss matters with you openly without walking on eggshells. After your introductory meeting, agree on the way you will communicate with each other (for instance, by email, a messaging app, or in person). When you write to teachers, keep your messages short and to the point. They are often busy and often have many parents to deal with, so long-winded emails are best avoided. Be patient for them to respond. Bear in mind that they may have many parents to contact, and they may be struggling to find a work-life balance.

Be as specific as possible with your requests, indicating the precise dates, actions, and responsibilities that need to be addressed, and don't be afraid to ask teachers for the reasons for their decisions. If you know a professional or have a close friend whom you feel can help advocate for your child, bring them along to meetings.

When you see your child's teachers, create a collaborative setting where you share key information so your child's needs can be addressed. Writer and specialist in Autism Sarah Hendrickx suggests bringing a photo of your child to any meeting about her education to remind others that she is a person, not just part of a program that is to be created cost-effectively (Hendrickx 2015). Finally, try to get teachers to set goals and rewards alongside your daughter and to ensure these goals are specific, achievable, and relatively short-range. Both the teacher and your child should also choose the rewards for achieving goals to keep motivation and interest high (Notbohm 2022).

End-of-Chapter Activity: Checklist for Selecting from Different School Options

When conducting your research into different school options and contacting your shortlist of schools, use the following checklist to help you weigh the pros and cons of each school (Gunner 2015):

- How many children in the school have Autism, and what range of needs do they have?
- How many students are in each class?
- What is the teacher-to-pupil ratio in each class?
- How is progress measured, and by whom?
- How often can parents access teachers and other staff, and by what means?
- What resources does the school have (for instance, sensory rooms, fidget toys, soft bean bags, and similar)?
- Are staff members trained in teaching Autistic students?
- How many student aides are currently helping students with Autism?
- What technology and resources are available at the school for children with Autism?
- How does the school accommodate sensory sensitivities in the classroom environment?

- What strategies are in place to support communication for nonverbal or minimally verbal Autistic students (if appropriate to your child)?
- How does the school help Autistic students with transitions between activities and classes?
- What social skills programs does the school offer?
- How does the school deal with bullying, social isolation, and sexual assault?
- What is the school's approach to IEPs and 504 plans?
- How does the school collaborate with external therapists or specialists working with Autistic students?
- What extracurricular activities or clubs are available that cater to the interests of Autistic students?
- How does the school handle meltdowns or behavioral challenges?
- How does the school view stimming?
- What accommodations are made for Autistic students during standardized testing? What about homework, assignments, and group work?
- How does the school support the development of life skills for Autistic students?
- How does the school facilitate peer interactions and friendships for Autistic students?

Once you have chosen a school for your child, the next step is to set up routines that help her strike a perfect balance between her academic, social, and family life. In Chapter 3, we will cover key routines for the morning, afternoon, and night.

R: ROUTINES THAT FOSTER SUCCESS

> *"Routine is a pivotal part of my daily life, and any deviation, however slight, can cause great discomfort to me."*
>
> — NATHAN CORNFIELD (MATUSIAK, N.D.)

Routines can help anyone feel more in control of their day and make them more effective time managers, but for Autistic people, they can be lifelines. When I look back to the early years of my childhood—when I was as young as four or five—I remember getting terribly upset when I was expecting my day to go a certain, predictable way and plans were suddenly shifted. For instance, if my parents told me we were going to the park, but it started raining, and they had to cancel, I would cry and insist on going anyway. My parents would explain that we couldn't use the swings or the slides, but our failure to go usually caused me considerable frustration. I still often feel that way when plans are suddenly changed. It's always a big effort to readjust when someone cancels an appointment or reschedules a social outing.

Establishing a routine for your child is vital because it enables her to follow familiar, comfortable patterns without the need to constantly process new information. Routines help kids navigate their lives with greater confidence and reduced stress and anxiety. They grant them a sense of control as they know how to prepare mentally and emotionally for an array of tasks, from getting to school to participating in an after-school club. They make Autistic kids feel safe and secure, and that means they can concentrate on pursuing their goals, strengthening their skills, and learning new things (Autism Specialty Group, n.d.).

Routines also allow children to become better time managers. When I was a student, I would use an alarm to remind myself of how long I had to complete homework tasks. That way, I had enough free time to go running and listen to music. If I didn't use a timer, I would sometimes take too long on one task and feel overwhelmed by all the other tasks I had to complete on a given day. Routines also helped me manage transitions between activities, which I found a bit challenging.

THE ELEMENTS OF A SUCCESSFUL ROUTINE

Morning, afternoon, and evening routines differ from household to household, but it is important to ensure that they contain the following elements (Adina ABA, n.d.):

- **Clearly Defined Tasks:** When creating your routine, instead of using wide terminology like "Get ready for bed," break tasks down into smaller, well-defined instructions such as "Put pajamas in the drawer," "Get dressed," "Brush teeth," "Put shoes on," and similar.
- **Body Doubling:** Autistic people can find it easier to complete a task when others are doing so alongside them. Other people can serve as a welcome distraction from sensory stimuli and make tough processes easier. For instance, I hate brushing my

teeth because there is so much sensory input to deal with—from touching the toothpaste cap to having to look in the mirror when I don't want to. What's more, I hate getting my wrists wet, so I have to concentrate on that, too. It's always like a race because I want to make sure I clean my teeth before the toothpaste gets too spicy in my mouth. Brushing my teeth with my daughters helps me dull the sensory stimuli, as they serve as distractions. I have lovely, clean teeth. I just hate the process involved in making them that way!

- **A Schedule with Steps:** Each task should be listed as a step and placed into a schedule your child can consult throughout the day. The schedule can be a list of tasks, a short video, or a visual board.
- **Continued Reference to the Schedule:** Pin your schedule in a visible spot and refer to it every time your child is about to begin a new task. This will help consolidate the information in her mind.
- **Consistent Application:** Complete every step in the routine and follow the established order. You may find it useful to use timers to ensure that steps are completed in time.
- **Consideration of Your Child's Sensory Needs:** Take your child's sensory sensitivities and preferences into account when creating your routine. For instance, if she finds loud noises challenging, she may benefit from using noise-canceling headphones while carrying out activities.
- **Break Times:** Schedule regular breaks or downtime so that your child has time to recharge and regulate her sensory systems. This can help prevent meltdowns and shutdowns.
- **Marked Transitions:** My wife Sarah and I find it really tough to move from one activity to the next. As a mother, I use songs to mark transitions between activities, both for myself and my kids. Sarah uses meal times to transition between different work tasks. She is a business owner, so there is always something to do, day or nighttime!

When I was a child, on weekends, my mom would plan the day around different shows on TV or ad breaks. I would eat breakfast while watching *The Wiggles*, and when that was over, I knew it was time to go outside. When *Playschool* came on, it was time to come inside and then do some reading. Parenting an Autistic kid can be very different from what you imagined, but by embracing routines and helping to smooth out transitions between activities, you will make your day a lot simpler for you and your child.

- **Flexibility:** Allow for some flexibility in your routine. For instance, if it's bedtime but your child is particularly engrossed in a task like reading or drawing, give her an extra ten minutes to finish her activity. This will prevent frustration and make the transition to bedtime a bit easier.

> *"I use a visual to-do list to show Naomi all the steps she needs to follow. I go over the next day's schedule with her before bed and again in the morning. This helps her feel more settled. Sometimes when we go out to, say, a restaurant, she has small meltdowns, so I am thinking about making visual schedules for leisure time activities as well."*
>
> — BEN, 27

> *"For my daughter Nadia's visual schedule, I print pictures of her daily activities and draw those I can't find pictures of. I paste the pictures over cardboard and laminate them, then attach a small Velcro dot to the back of the pictures. I also use a 2" x 3" grid whiteboard with times written on it and stick Velcro dots in the time slots. This system allows me to change my child's schedule easily."*
>
> — SANNI, 33

TOOLS FOR CREATING A ROUTINE

As a teacher, I have always loved finding new technology and tools to help my students (and myself) stay focused and organized. Below is a list of favorites among kids and parents that may come in handy when you're creating routines alongside your child:

- **CoPilot by Goally:** This app allows you to make custom charts, checklists, and first-then boards. Each activity comes with pictures, video, audio, and timers, and kids get rewards for doing their work. The app has various task categories that it divides into steps. For instance, it has a guide containing each step your child needs to get dressed, with pictures of each step.

  Your child can click "Listen," and the app will read each step out loud. For instance, it helps kids get dressed by telling them to put on their underwear, then their shirt, pants, socks, shoes, and so forth. A blue circle jumps from one task to another to motivate the child to complete the step and move on to the next one.

  There are also interactive tutorials that show kids how to complete each task—for instance, putting their shoes on. Your child can also click the "Practice" button, which allows users to practice a task independently (for instance, putting on their T-shirt) within a set amount of time, with visual aids to boot. When kids complete a task, they earn points or puzzle pieces they can redeem for rewards determined by parents in the app or for game time. The app aims to create useful habit loops. Children learn a new skill by watching a short video, then rehearse the skill with their parents, practice the skill, and obtain points for their commitment.

- **Choiceworks:** This app is similar to CoPilot in that it helps children complete daily routines. It also contains visuals aimed at helping them regulate their emotions and improve patience-related skills such as waiting and turn-taking. It has an image library with over 180 images and audio files, and if you wish, you can add your own images for ultimate personalization.

    You can save an unlimited number of boards for multiple children and different routines. The app speaks your boards out loud with a child or adult voice and has custom timer sounds. It also allows you to print and share your boards via email and iTunes.

- **Time Trackers:** There are so many visual timers, and, of course, you can always use a free timer on your phone to help your child complete tasks in a timely fashion. One device that is really popular with parents I know is Time Timer, a visual timer that eases stressful transitions by showing kids how much longer they have to complete a task. Parents find this tool useful because it has a red countdown that gets smaller and smaller, making time seem like a less abstract concept. Bear in mind, however, that timers don't work for everyone! They give me anxiety because I can't help but constantly look at the clock, waiting for the time to run out. Let your child choose the tools and devices that help her progress.
- **Whiteboards:** In the testimonial section above, you saw how Sanni uses her own whiteboard system, which is cheap and easy to customize. Sanni recommends a 2" x 3" whiteboard grid because it is big enough to accommodate good-quality photos and drawings. You can do like Sanni and use Velcro to stick images onto the whiteboard, or use a magnetic whiteboard and attach images onto it with magnetic clips (these are cheap and easily available on Amazon and other online stores).

- **Push Button Light Walls:** One tool many parents call a total game-changer is a simple yet super-effective way to get kids excited about following routines. It involves pasting images indicating tasks to be completed on the wall and sticking push button lights beneath each task. These lights run on a battery and come in a range of colors. Every time your child completes a task, she can push the light and watch it turn on. One parent I know has different sets of lights depending on the room. For instance, next to the main door, she has photographs of her child's knapsack, water bottle, lunch box, shoes, and coat, with words written beneath the images and a push light beneath the words. As her daughter completes each task (for instance, taking her lunch from the fridge and putting it into her knapsack), she pushes the light beneath it. She knows she's ready to exit the door and head to the school bus when all items are lit up.

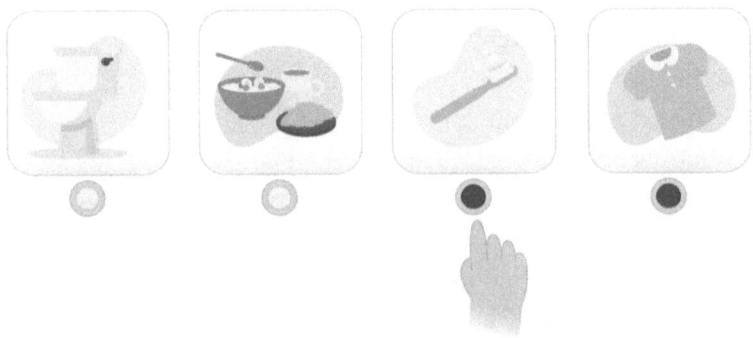

SETTING UP YOUR CHILD'S DAILY ROUTINES

Every child's morning routine may be slightly different, but sample routines for the morning, afternoon, and evening can comprise the following activities, which I have broken down into simple steps:

In the Morning

- Waking Up:
  - Turning off the alarm
  - Getting out of bed
  - Making the bed
  - Putting on her slippers
- Completing Personal Hygiene Tasks:
  - Washing her face
  - Brushing her teeth
  - Combing her hair
- Getting Dressed:
  - Taking off her pajama top and bottom and her underwear
  - Putting on new underwear
  - Putting on her shirt/top/dress
  - Putting on her shorts/skirt
  - Putting on her socks/stockings
  - Putting on her shoes
  - Putting her pajama top, bottom, and nighttime underwear in the wash basket
- Having Breakfast:
  - Sitting at the table
  - Eating breakfast
  - Taking her dishes back to the sink/placing her dishes in the dishwasher
- Getting Ready for School:
  - Taking her water bottle and placing it in her knapsack
  - Taking her lunch from the fridge and placing it in her knapsack
  - Putting on her coat

I suggest that you utilize either an app like CoPilot or various whiteboards placed strategically—for instance, in her bedroom and in the bathroom, kitchen/dining area, and foyer.

In the Afternoon

- Getting Back from School:
    - Entering the door, taking off her coat, and hanging it on the coat rack
    - Placing her lunch box and drink bottle in the kitchen
    - Sitting down at the table
    - Having a snack
- Doing Her Homework:
    - Taking her schoolwork and sitting down at her desk
    - Looking at her list of homework activities
    - Starting with the earliest task that is due
    - Doing a bit of extra reading
- Leisure Time:
    - Playing on her tablet for half an hour
    - Going for a walk with a parent and a pet
    - Playing music for half an hour

In the Evening

- Having Dinner:
    - Washing her hands
    - Helping parents set the table
    - Sitting down to dine
    - Talking about her day with her family
    - Taking the dishes back to the sink or dishwasher
- Taking a Bath:
    - Taking off her shirt
    - Taking off her shorts/skirt
    - Taking off her underwear
    - Getting in the bath
    - Applying bath gel to her sponge and cleaning her body
    - Applying shampoo
    - Rinsing off the soap and shampoo

- Drying herself with a towel
    - Combing her hair
    - Putting on underwear
    - Putting on her pajama top
    - Putting on her pajama pants
- Getting Ready for Bed:
    - Getting in bed
    - Reading a book
    - Doing a body scan or short breathing or mindfulness meditation session
    - Turning off the night light

Be prepared for tiring nights when your child gets up numerous times and asks you for everything under the sun. It won't always happen, but my own childhood tells me that it can! That's why ensuring that sport is part of her daily routine can be a big help, as can anything that gets her tired!

A NOTE ON SLEEP

Sleep can be a bit of a challenge for children with Autism because many run through their day at nighttime to process all the events they have experienced (Hendrickx 2015). Numerous studies have shown that Autistic girls have been found to have more bedtime resistance, sleep anxiety, daytime sleep, and less overall sleep than boys (Estes et al. 2022). As a whole, it is thought that the reasons why Autistic kids may struggle with sleep more than their neurotypical peers include:

- Difficulties winding down
- Frequent waking during the night
- Anxiety or difficulties relaxing, which can lead to insomnia
- Social cueing issues, or not making a connection between others going to bed and their own need to sleep
- Sensory difficulties, such as heightened sensitivity to blue light from phones, tablets, and other screens

- Food allergies, which can cause gastrointestinal upset
- Stress, which can lead to oversleeping

To help your child get a good night's sleep, start by designing a bedroom that is conducive to sleepiness. Use blackout curtains and soundproof her room if you can, or reduce noise levels by closing doors and fitting your child's room with thick carpeting. Remove distractions such as gadgets and pictures on the wall, and ensure she has comfy, soft pajamas without tags.

Consider diffusing therapeutic-grade lavender essential oil, which has been found in numerous studies to reduce stress (Sattayakhom 2023). If your child enjoys guided meditation, read them a script that can help them relax and forget about the day's worries. Some children may simply prefer that you read them a book.

Ensure your child stops using screens at least an hour before bed, as the blue light from tablets and other screens can keep kids alert when the aim is for them to feel sleepy (Schulze 2022). My experience with Autism has shown me that sometimes, kids with a combination of Autism and ADHD may need a little screen time in the evening as a way to calm down. Others prefer to have a little active play (say pillow fighting or play wrestling) before bed to calm down because they need to feel exhausted to feel sleepy. When it comes to routines, let your child's preferences lead the way because a routine that is perfect for one child may not suit another child at all.

DETERMINING A HEALTHY AMOUNT OF SCREEN TIME FOR YOUR CHILD

When I was at school, I remember wishing I had my laptop or tablet with me during lunchtime. I made it a point to spend breaks with the other girls when I could manage it, but secretly yearned to be alone, surfing for rock music tunes or looking for information about my hobbies. As it turns out, I wasn't alone. It is now well-known that kids with Autism tend to spend more time engaging with screen content than their neurotypical peers. One study found that boys with Autism watch an average of 2.9 hours of TV daily, compared to 2.3 hours for neurotypical boys. Autistic girls, meanwhile, averaged three hours compared to two hours for neurotypical girls. They also spent longer on screens such as tablets than neurotypical peers. Girls with Autism, in particular, show a high level of engagement on social media and video chat activities, spending around 45.5 minutes on these platforms vs. 21.9 minutes for neurotypical girls (Must et al. 2023).

This information is a reminder of why it is so important to help your child manage her screen time. I mentioned creating schedules, but you may also find it useful to create a designated "screen use zone" for your kids. For instance, you can set a rule stating that they can only use their screens in your living room. This will ensure they don't spend hours chatting or surfing while they are in bed. I also suggest monitoring your children's screen use and managing their passwords to ensure the pages they visit are child-appropriate.

Finally, help your child empower herself through self-monitoring. It is important for her to understand that excessive screen time is linked to problems like anxiety and depression and that it can stop her from getting a good night's sleep (Berthold 2024). Show her a few tools that can help her manage her screen use. Apps like Apple Screen Time allow users to set daily limits on how much time they spend on specific apps, categories of apps, or their phone in general. Google Family Link is similar, and it works on both iPhone and Android.

When your child turns thirteen, switch to an app like Qustodio, which allows users to set time limits and create multiple schedules, as well as block calls. Unlike Family Link, Qustodio allows users to block out more than one time period (such as dinner time and bedtime) (Wirecutter 2024).

PREPARING YOUR CHILD FOR CHANGES TO HER ROUTINE

If you know your child will be taking part in a new activity, meeting new people, or going to a new place or on a school field trip, try to prepare her as much as you can beforehand. You can do this by:

- Incorporate the change into her schedule and go over it various times so she knows what to expect. Remember to break up the activity into many smaller segments so your child feels a sense of control over what is going to take place.
- Use social stories that show the social situations your child may encounter during the field trip. For instance, she may meet new activity leaders, be asked to form part of a group, or take part in sports or creative activities. The stories should indicate all these steps and be told many times so your child has a firm grasp on them.
- Arrange visits to new places during quiet times so she has a chance to get used to them. For instance, if you know your child will be visiting an art gallery with her schoolmates, try making a family visit to the gallery beforehand so she becomes familiar with her surroundings.
- Make slow changes and add new activities one at a time if possible. Doing so will make it easier for her to process change.
- Enlist the help of your teachers if your child is going on a field trip. For instance, your child may prefer to sit with a friend or her teacher at the front of the bus or wear noise-canceling headphones. Share her sensory needs and preferences with her school so that the staff is prepared to make the experience as enriching as possible.
- Ask your child's school if your child can have a peer buddy.
- Consider attending as a volunteer.
- Ask the teacher if your child can have a task or job to fulfill.

Aside from these strategies, I also advise you to practice what to do when things go "wrong." It can help if your child is prepared for situations such as sensory overload, a teacher moving the class to a new spot, or someone being mean. Role-plays can be an excellent way to "pretend" that one of these situations has occurred. They can help your child feel the kind of emotions she may encounter in real life. That way, she can have a "plan of action," which can include everything from putting on her headphones to asking the teacher if she can go to the bathroom for a while. Try to notice the strategies your child prefers and share them with her teacher.

End-of-Chapter Activity: Creating a Sleep Kit for Your Child

Create a "sleep kit" that you can use to help your child relax at bedtime. Below, you will find three ideas to add to the kit, though I hope you add many more relaxing activities as the days and weeks go by!

- **Bedtime Star Breathing:** Controlled breathing has been found in numerous studies to curb stress and anxiety. In my first book, I shared four powerful breathing exercises, but here's one more they may enjoy completing at nighttime!
    - Invite your child to sit or lie on her bed. Tell her to close her eyes and imagine that she is looking up at a starry night.
    - Invite her to breathe in the starlight by taking a big, slow breath in through her nose while she slowly counts to three.
    - Ask her to "hold the sparkle" (or hold the breath in) and count to two, imagining that her breath is filling her body with a sparkly glow.
    - Now, invite her to "blow out the stardust" by slowly breathing out through her mouth and imagining that she is sending soft stardust floating into the night sky. Ask her to count to four as she blows the air out.

- Repeat the exercise as many times as your child wishes, and ask her to notice if she feels calmer.
- Invite her to let her body relax more and more with each breath until she is ready to drift off to sleep like a star floating into a soft cloud.
- **A Mindfulness Meditation Script to Read to Your Child at Bedtime:** Consider reading this mindfulness meditation script to your child to help her feel more like sleeping:
    - Close your eyes and imagine you are lying on a soft, fluffy cloud. Take a slow, deep breath in through your nose as if you're breathing in the fresh, pure air of the sky. Now, breathe out gently through your mouth, like a breeze passing through the clouds. Feel your body getting lighter, like it's sinking gently into your cloud. Wiggle your toes once, then let them rest. Now, imagine your legs becoming as soft and light as the cloud you're on. Feel your belly rise and fall with each breath, calm and peaceful. Let your arms feel weightless like they're floating. Let the cloud carry you slowly across the sky, rocking you gently. There's nothing you need to do, nowhere you need to go—just relax and let the cloud hold you. You are safe, cozy, and ready to drift into sleep. Sweet dreams.
- **Leaves on a Stream Exercise for De-Stressing:** This exercise is taken from Acceptance and Commitment Therapy, which seeks to help people accept the challenges in their lives while committing to making positive change (Cleveland Clinic, n.d.). You can use this exercise to teach your child how to handle intrusive thoughts when she is trying to go to bed.
    - Invite your child to sit in a comfy position on her bed and close her eyes or rest them gently on a fixed spot.
    - Ask her to visualize herself walking by a peaceful stream with leaves floating on it. Pause for a few seconds and invite her to work out the details of this scene—the season of the year it is, the color of the leaves, the sound of the water, and the feel of the grass, leaves, or tree bark.

- Invite her to think of the thoughts that are running through her mind and to place each thought on a leaf.
- Ask her to imagine that these "thought leaves" are gently flowing by. Some may take a while longer to move along, while others may easily glide by.
- Tell her that if her mind tells her things like, "This activity is hard," or "This is dumb," she can place those thoughts on leaves, too!
- Let her know that when difficult thoughts arise, she can say, "I am having a feeling of boredom/frustration/impatience," and place those thoughts on a leaf.
- Share that if, once in a while, thoughts distract her from the exercise, that is perfectly okay. She can take a deep breath and go back to the stream at any time.

In this chapter, I have shared tips for setting routines for your child and keeping your eye on her screen time. In the next chapter, we will dive into one of the most important aspects of your daughter's time in school: her learning journey.

L: LEARNING STRATEGIES FOR ACADEMIC GROWTH

> *"To be yourself in a world that is constantly trying to make you somethig else is the greatest accomplishment."*
>
> — RALPH WALDO EMERSON (YELLOW BUS ABA 2024)

Girls with Autism often face daily challenges that can make it harder for them to learn—including difficulties with understanding instructions, filtering out noises and other distractions, dealing with transitions, and keeping up with the pace established by the teacher. All these reasons are precisely why it is so important to meet your child where she is at instead of trying to force her to fit into an academic mold that is made for a different type of brain.

In this chapter, I'd like to share a few strategies that helped me in my academic journey, as well as those that have served Autistic girls and women in my community. I mentioned at the start that being in class was always stressful and energy-draining for me because the teacher always seemed to be going too fast and transitions were a nightmare. However, I relied on a small but effective list of strategies that enabled me to achieve my dream of becoming a teacher. I knew exactly what I wanted to study and concentrated on building the knowledge that would get me into my chosen university.

While I was in class, I decided to simply survive instead of trying to process all the information shared by my teachers. I did all my learning by myself at home, in my sensorially friendly environment. One of the strategies that worked best for me was to obtain print-outs of my teachers' PowerPoint slides. In class, I would write the topic of the lesson in my book and then just sit and listen and be well-behaved. Upon arriving home, I would devour books like *Encyclopedia Britannica* and research my work on what was then a very primitive version of the internet. I would use search engines like Ask Jeeves to learn more about the topics being taught in class. I actually enjoyed studying this way because it meant that I wasn't getting in trouble at school and I could still learn things. Likewise, I loved discovering facts that the teacher hadn't shared in class, like how Ancient Egypt had a ten-day week. I would bring that knowledge to the classroom on days when I was feeling confident. Because I wasn't diagnosed until I was thirty, teacher support was few and far between, and I had to rely on myself. If you obtain an Autism diagnosis for your child, you will be able to rely on an IEP or 504 Plan, which allows your child to learn in a more personalized way.

RECOGNIZING DIFFERENT LEARNING STYLES

In her book *Women and Girls with Autism Spectrum Disorder*, Sarah Hendrickx, who is Autistic, writes that at school, she was often described as "lazy" by teachers for not achieving top grades despite being a gifted-level student. "I have always said that I knew the answer, but I didn't know the question. It was other people's language I had trouble with, not my own," she says, adding that verbal and written language processing were always a challenge. She adds that Autistic girls and boys often show unusual, uneven learning profiles, with extreme highs and lows (Hendrickx 2015). This can be attributed to various causes, such as the cognitive challenges of Autism, the way a student processes information, the teacher's style, and the student's level of interest and motivation.

Autistic people may use their logic and conclude that if they aren't "good" at something, then they shouldn't even bother trying to do it. This is why sometimes, making a small change (such as relating a topic in class to a child's special interest) can make a big difference to a child's learning experience.

THE IMPORTANCE OF DIFFERENTIATED INSTRUCTION

In his book *How the Brain Learns*, author David Sousa states that understanding the diverse learning needs of students based on neurological differences is key in modern education (Sousa 2016). In essence, everyone's brain is unique; they have different neural pathways and processing abilities. By recognizing these differences, teachers and parents can help children achieve their full potential.

In her book *Ten Things Every Child with Autism Wishes You Knew*, Ellen Notbohm writes that children with Autism can take an individual path to learning (Notbohm 2022). Some take a sequential approach, preferring to learn things in a step-by-step manner. They typically enjoy learning from textbooks, following tutorials, or attending lectures because these methods show them the path they need to follow (Funderstanding 2024). Other children take a more global approach, looking at the "big picture" first. They like to see how all parts fit together and focus on connections and the entire idea instead of on tiny details. For instance, a child might prefer to learn a whole phrase and repeat it (echolalia), then break down the phrase and learn the meaning of individual words (Yacoub 2023).

VARK LEARNING STYLES AND GARDNER'S THEORY OF MULTIPLE INTELLIGENCES

Most parents agree that their children enjoy learning things in more than one way. Exploring your child's preferences is invaluable because research shows that children who are more engaged learn more (Outschool, n.d.). In 1987, Neil Fleming created a learning style model based on the sensory modalities of learning. It comprised four learning styles (Cherry 2024):

- **Visual:** Those with this learning style have a preference for pictures, films, and diagrams.
- **Auditory:** People who enjoy auditory learning enjoy learning information through music, lectures, and discussions.
- **Reading and Writing:** Those who prefer the reading and writing learning style enjoy reading textbooks, taking notes, and making lists.
- **Kinesthetic:** People with a kinesthetic learning style enjoy hands-on activities such as dance, sports, and experiments.

An individual's learning style determines the type of information they find more enjoyable and easier to process. For instance, visual learners may enjoy viewing photographs, videos, symbols, written instructions, diagrams, graphic organizers, and miniatures of real objects. Auditory learners may consolidate their learning via repetition, verbal discourse, recorded lessons, reading material aloud, and playing background music. Kinesthetic learners may prefer to learn outdoors, perform experiments, make models, use sensory devices, and take breaks so they can move their bodies. Finally, those favoring the reading and writing style may learn by taking notes, writing essays or stories, or participating in written discussions using a discussion board. The latter allows students to post information and receive written replies instead of expressing themselves verbally (Fitzgerald 2023).

The VARK model was instrumental in demonstrating the importance of individualized learning strategies. However, it focused mainly on how people absorb information without taking into account a broader spectrum of students' cognitive and emotional abilities. Howard Gardner's theory of Multiple Intelligences widened the scope, providing us with a more nuanced perspective of human interests and abilities. Gardner's theory embraces nine types of intelligence (Cherry 2023):

- **Visual-Spatial Intelligence:** Individuals with high visual-spatial intelligence are good with directions, recognizing patterns, and reading maps and charts. They may enjoy drawing, painting, reading, and writing in their leisure time and may be good at interpreting pictures and graphs (Cherry 2023).
- **Linguistic-Verbal Intelligence:** People who are strong in this type of intelligence tend to be good at expressing themselves both in writing and when speaking. They are usually able to write engaging stories and memorize information, and they enjoy reading.
- **Logical-Mathematical:** Those with high logical-mathematical intelligence excel at recognizing patterns, analyzing problems logically, and reasoning. They enjoy thinking about abstract ideas, solving problems, and completing challenging computations.
- **Kinesthetic Learning:** Individuals with high kinesthetic intelligence are good at physical control and body movement. They have optimal hand-eye coordination and dexterity and often excel in activities such as dance or sports. They tend to remember things by doing them rather than hearing about or seeing them.
- **Musical Intelligence:** People who have strong musical intelligence enjoy thinking in patterns, rhythms, and sounds. They may excel at musical composition and performance and love singing or playing instruments (Frothingham 2024).
- **Interpersonal Intelligence:** Those with high interpersonal intelligence excel at conflict resolution, communication, and seeing situations from different perspectives. They tend to create positive relationships with others and are skilled at both verbal and nonverbal language.

- **Intrapersonal Intelligence:** People with strong intrapersonal intelligence are aware of their emotional states, thoughts, and motivations. They enjoy thinking about their strengths and identifying areas for improvement. They also take pleasure in analyzing theories and ideas.
- **Naturalist Intelligence:** People with naturalistic intelligence often feel deeply connected to nature. They may have a profound interest in plants, wildlife, rocks, camping, hiking, and other outdoor activities.
- **Existential Intelligence:** Those with strong existential intelligence can see the big picture, and they have a long-term outlook on things. They consider how current actions can affect the future and have the ability to see things "from the outside."

Some academics have criticized Gardner's approach because it lacks conclusive scientific evidence to support the independence of different intelligences. Neuroscience actually suggests that cognitive functions are interconnected, not modular. The theory also lacks standardized tools to measure different types of intelligence reliably (Waterhouse 2023).

However, Gardner's theory is loved by many teachers because it highlights the importance of tapping into the type of learning activities that children enjoy. For instance, if your child loves nature and enjoys studying plants and wildlife, watching birds, or foraging, it pays to give her many opportunities to do so. A child with naturalistic intelligence will undoubtedly enjoy learning more about the plant and animal world by being in the thick of a lush forest than by simply reading information about it in a book.

To identify your child's preferred learning styles and intelligences, observe her strengths and interests, as well as the type of tasks or information she finds most challenging. Look at the way she communicates and analyzes her sensory preferences. Observe how she focuses, and ask her questions to discover more about how she enjoys learning.

Try to make learning as enjoyable and fascinating as you can for your child. If your focus is constantly on comparing her progress to that of other kids, chances are, she will feel your frustration and sense that in your eyes, she "just isn't good enough." By tapping into her strengths and interests, you can help her feel like she excels in her areas of interest.

Keep your eye on your child and ignore others' comments, criticisms, and judgments. Remember that many of her core beliefs and values will come from you. You can help her see herself as a wonderful, brilliant, curious kid who can dedicate her life to things and people she feels passionate about. She doesn't have to learn everything right now, nor does she have to keep up with anyone else. Support her by exercising patience, being open-minded, and offering her as many opportunities as you can to learn new things, meet new people, and embark on exciting adventures.

SHARING YOUR CHILD'S SPECIAL INTERESTS WITH TEACHERS

Special interests, defined by the Autistic Advocacy Network as being "narrow and deep," are prevalent among Autistic people; between 75 and 95 percent of us have them. One study has found that Autistic children typically have around nine special interests, with the mean age of onset being 5.24 years (Laber-Warren 2021).

Sharing your daughter's special interests with her teachers is a great way to keep her motivated and inspired. Most teachers are busy, and they may not be able to personalize classes to the extent they wish they could. However, there are many ways that they can motivate your child without veering too far from their lesson plans. For instance, say your child loves music. If she is learning about history in class, instead of being asked to write an essay, she may enjoy playing a piece of music from that historical era. If she loves being out in nature, instead of simply writing about local ecosystems, she may enjoy handing in a photo log of her last visit to a forest or seaside area. If she's into math, instead of writing about global warming, she may wish to put together a mathematical representation of how much energy families can save by embracing green lifestyle habits.

Research by Tony Attwood has shown that Autistic girls often have special interests that are typical for girls their age, such as watching TV, following social media channels and influencers, riding horses, or collecting dolls (Attwood 2007). Other areas of interest may include (Autism Awareness Australia, n.d.-b):

- Nature
- Animals
- Celebrities
- Historical figures
- Fiction and science fiction
- Plush toys
- Collecting things
- Anime
- Gaming
- Psychology
- Social toys

However, girls may also have interests that are not typically "female." In general, both Autistic girls and boys engage less in spontaneous "pretend play" than their neurotypical peers (Healis Autism Centre 2021). Examples of pretend play include having tea parties, animating dolls, using a random item as a "phone," or pretending a box is a treehouse. When playing games that do not involve pretending, Autistic girls enjoy games and toys such as Legos, robots, and activities involving organizing rather than imagining things. However, when they *do* play pretend games, they show a preference for typically female toys and games, possibly because they are taught these games at home or in school. They may also have imaginary friends (Knickmeyer et al. 2007).

FOSTERING YOUR CHILD'S SPECIAL INTERESTS OUTSIDE SCHOOL

You may not be able to control the extent to which your daughter's teachers cater to her preferences, but there is plenty you can do after school and on weekends. For instance, you can immerse yourself in your child's special interests and share information and resources with her. She will most probably enjoy having someone who shares her passions, and the more you dive into a topic, the more likely you are to enjoy discussing your findings with her.

In my first book, I shared ideas for encouraging your child to pursue her special interests. These include giving her your full attention while she is talking about her special interests, creating a project alongside her, and seeing unfinished projects as a valid and useful way for her to spend time. It is okay for children to start a project and lose interest midway. Remember that these activities help them relieve stress and add to their knowledge bank. There are many ways to tap into your child's interests, including volunteering, creating books or scrapbooks, and joining online and in-person clubs. Let your child lead the way, and you'll always have a rich source of ideas!

HOW TO HELP YOUR CHILD PREPARE FOR TESTS AND ASSESSMENTS

Throughout my school and university years, tests and assessments were always a major source of stress, especially because we were given a limited time to complete all questions and there were often many instructions to follow. Of course, I had no idea at the time that feelings like anxiety, sensory overwhelm, or a literal understanding of questions, all of which affected how I answered questions, were common to Autism (National Autistic Society, n.d.-b). As I got older, especially at university, exams could last for hours, and it was tough to stay focused and manage my time well to ensure I answered all the questions on the test.

Lack of motivation is another major obstacle for many Autistic boys and girls. Children may not understand *why* they need to complete an exam when they are confident that they know the subject matter. This was very much the case for me when I had to study for a test or write an essay on a subject that had nothing to do with what I wanted to study. In high school, I knew that I had to do well enough to be admitted to university to complete my teaching degree. However, if a subject had no impact on my job path, I wasn't worried about failing, and I wouldn't study for it.

Still, motivation and results are a two-way street. The better your child does at tests and exams, the less likely she is to fear them. Make sure she gets to do many practice exams. This is one task that teachers can help out with. I would suggest asking teachers for test formats beforehand so you can practice for the style of test, whether it has a question-and-answer or multiple-choice type format. As your child gets older, she may have more essay-type exams, and each question may have a specific number of marks. Show her how to spend more time on questions with a higher value, perhaps by using a stopwatch initially and then just a wristwatch. Note that some kids may find watches overwhelming, so go with what feels comfortable for her.

Throughout the school year, encourage your child to prepare way ahead for exams and tests through the method that works best for her. It might be useful to ask her teacher for the test and exam schedule so you can keep track of when they are coming up. I shared my preference for researching topics myself at home or rewriting the teacher's notes and using pictures to help me understand and memorize the content. You can do so by helping her access or create images, photographs, flashcards, and vocabulary key rings.

When tests or exams are coming up, start preparing early and break topics up into smaller chunks. For instance, if a test covers one chapter in her textbook and the chapter has, say, eight units, suggest that she should work on just one or two units a day for four or five days. At the end of study sessions, she can set aside five to ten minutes to revise the units she covered the day before. That way, it will be easier to learn key information. Remind her to spend the last day or two before the test revising the content she already knows. You can either create a mock exam yourself or access past tests or exams from teachers. You can also ask and answer questions orally if your child prefers revising this way.

Allow her to revise in the way that works best for her. She may have a preferred time, environment, or technique for studying. I mentioned that I worked best alone, but some kids may enjoy studying for exams with a buddy. As she gets older, she may prefer to study without your help. If so, let her know that you are there to offer support and access to resources. If she needs a tutor in a tricky subject, give her access to an online or in-person tutor if possible. Share any findings you make regarding new visual supports or memory aids that may align with her learning style, but let her take the lead regarding the resources she prefers to use.

> *"When studying for exams, I used to line up my stuffed toys and 'teach' them the subject I was studying. It helped me to say the words out loud, and having my toys there made me feel comforted."*
>
> — JULIANNE, 19

> *"My mother helped me study from a very young age by showing me how to make mnemonics and songs to remember lists and other information for tests. She used to also help me make mind maps, which helped me remember things like historical events or topics for science, like plant anatomy."*
>
> — GILDA, 41

HELPING YOUR CHILD DEVELOP A CONFIDENT MINDSET

It can be harder to perform well and concentrate on exactly what tests and exams are asking if one is stressed. That is why it is important to help your child feel confident about exams and to teach her techniques that can help curb stress and anxiety. Earlier, I shared a breathing exercise your child can use when they are feeling stressed out before a test. Another way to help her feel more comfortable with tests is to create social stories centered on the topic of exams. These stories show the series of actions that take place in a given situation, helping your child feel more in control of what is taking place.

Physical activity is more essential than it seems. In my first book, I explained how running was a real lifeline for me because it enabled me to shake off the immense stress I felt from spending hours a day masking. Study after study has shown that physical activity can reduce stress and anxiety for Autistic people (Riis et al. 2024). Let your child choose the exercise she enjoys the most, from yoga to football, horseback riding, or swimming, and model self-care behaviors by working out regularly by yourself or as a family.

SPECIAL ARRANGEMENTS FOR YOUR CHILD DURING EXAMS

Schools are allowed to make arrangements for Autistic students to help them demonstrate their knowledge during tests and exams. These include:

- Giving kids extended time
- Providing separate testing rooms
- Allowing them to use computers/type instead of writing their answers by hand
- Offering kids breaks during testing
- Offering alternative test formats

- Allowing them to use stim toys, listen to music, or access alternative media

Parents can play a key role in ensuring these arrangements are made for their children by establishing a close relationship with teachers and freely asking for accommodations that will help their children feel more secure.

HELPING YOUR CHILD DEAL WITH SETBACKS

As hard as your child prepares for tests and exams, she may not receive the grades she had hoped for. Help her deal with disappointment by encouraging her to embrace a growth mindset and see mistakes and "failures" as opportunities for growth. For instance, if she gets a math problem wrong, she can decide to complete many similar problems until she "cracks the code" and finds this type of problem easy.

As a parent, you are the key to ensuring that her self-esteem isn't eroded by disappointing results. There are many ways you can make her feel accepted, including rewarding her for her effort (*not* for her results). Avoid taking away her comfort items. Remember that routine (including hobbies like watching a favorite TV show when they get back from school) helps Autistic kids de-stress from the academic and social stressors they may face at school. Avoid obsessing over academic performance. If your child doesn't do well in a test, leave it for a few days, then, during a calm moment, try to find out the answers to questions such as:

- Is the teacher explaining things too fast?
- Is your child not paying attention because she doesn't feel the subject is useful to her or relevant to what she wants to do in the future?
- Is she at a more advanced level than her peers because the subject covers her special interest?
- Is social anxiety stopping her from participating?
- Is school so stressful that when she gets home, she wants to have zero to do with the subjects she is studying?

Knowing *why* your child is struggling is a vital way to find the help they need and even reconsider the school they are going to. Perhaps she will benefit by having subjects explained in the context of areas that interest her. She may need more time to reflect on topics and may be overwhelmed if she is expected to process everything the minute the teacher shares information. Perhaps the problem is the way her classmates or teachers are treating her. Listen to her actively, with an open mind, and with all your attention. Make sure she feels understood and assume that if she doesn't do something she is asked at school or in a test, it's because she *can't* do so, not because she doesn't *want* to.

End-of-Chapter Activity: Social Stories for Test Time

Write three to five social stories to help your child prepare for exams, illustrating each step or thought with an image. These could cover:

- What exams are
- How to revise before the exam
- What to do right before an exam
- What happens during exams

Below is a sample social story of what exams are (National Autistic Society, n.d.-b):

On some days, teachers give students tests so students can demonstrate their knowledge. You can have a test in any subject, such as math, English, or science. When a teacher tells you that you will have a test, they usually tell you what the test will be about. It is helpful to listen to what they say so you know what to focus on. Sometimes, students can feel nervous before an exam. It is okay to feel nervous. They can do activities like breathing to feel calmer.

In this chapter, we have discussed ways to help your child learn. The next chapter is closely related because it covers a subject that can also make her learning journey easier and more enjoyable: knowing how to tackle sensory challenges.

: SENSORY SUCCESS

> "Autism is not a disease. Don't try to cure us. Try to understand us."
>
> — BRIAN R. KING (ADVANCED AUTISM SERVICES 2024)

One of the hardest sensory challenges for me at school was all the talking that took place throughout the day. I have a limit for how much sensory input I can take, and when it is surpassed, words flow out of my brain like water overflowing from a glass. It can get frustrating when the noise won't stop, and one way that I deal with that is to shut down and become silent. My experiences in childhood and adulthood showed me that successful solutions for Autistic girls and women won't necessarily be the same as those that work for neurotypical girls.

One common misconception is that when children are overwhelmed, the only thing that works is calming them down so they can continue to receive more stimuli. I found it more effective to go into my own little world. Doing this enabled me to self-regulate and continue to enjoy the perks of being a "good kid" in class. I think if I hadn't temporarily switched off, it would have been impossible to stop myself from yelling and/or becoming very distressed. My childhood experiences have shown me how important it is to allow each child to soothe herself in the way that works best for her.

HOW SENSORY CHALLENGES CAN IMPACT LEARNING

Between 70 and 96 percent of Autistic children have some difficulties with sensory processing. Hyperactivity or hypo-reactivity to sensory input or unusual interests in sensory aspects is one of the four types of restrictive, repetitive patterns used to diagnose ASD (Piller and Barimo 2019). A child who is hyper-reactive to sensory input responds to sensory information that is not typically noticed by others, while a child who is hypo-reactive may not respond to sensory input typically noticed by others. For instance, a child who is hyper-reactive may cover their ears when someone is talking at a loud volume. A child who is hypo-reactive, meanwhile, may not respond to sounds that others find uncomfortable. For example, they might turn the volume on the television up very high or not notice when someone calls their name from across the room. When a child is hyper-reactive, they can be in a constant state of high alert, which makes it difficult for them to pay attention. In contrast, a child who is hypo-reactive does not receive the sensory input their body needs, and they may seek this input through behaviors that interfere with learning activities in the classroom.

Sensory processing challenges can lead to decreased participation in academic tasks, social activities, sporting activities, play, and self-care. It can also compromise a child's ability to pay attention, which is a pillar of communication and language development. In some cases, it can contribute to self-injury and aggressive behaviors, especially when children are unable to communicate their difficulties (Ashburner et al. 2008). I certainly know what this feels like since, at times, I was so frustrated that I felt like lashing out at my teacher, peers, or anyone. It was hard enough to have to pay attention to everything the teacher was saying, let alone to understand myself and relate to others in my environment.

CREATING A SENSORY MAP

You can help your child overcome sensory difficulties by engaging the services of an occupational therapist (OT). A qualified OT typically forms part of an interprofessional team that can include a speech-language pathologist or SLP (also called a speech therapist) and other professionals. The American Occupational Therapy Association recommends that sensory-based recommendations be implemented after an OT assesses a child's sensory processing(Piller et al. 2019). Some ways that an OT can work to help your child include:

- **Movement/Vestibular Input:** The vestibular system, located in the inner ears, helps you regulate your sense of balance and body control. When it isn't working very well, it can impede your understanding of what is happening to you and the world around you.

Movement or vestibular input exercises focus on vertical movements such as jumping. They can also comprise slow linear movements like using a rocking chair or swinging in a hammock. Finally, they can include controlled spinning activities, balancing, or jumping activities to enhance sensory input and integration (Apex ABA Therapy 2024a).

- **Proprioceptive Input:** Proprioception is the perception or awareness of the position and movement of the body. A simple way to think of it is as "the body awareness sense." It tells us where our body parts are without having to look for them and helps us know where body parts are relative to each other, honing our coordination skills (Pathways.org, n.d.). It also tells us how much force to use when we're holding, lifting, pushing, or pulling objects. Some people with Autism can have difficulty with the sense of proprioception, and they may do things like stand too close to others, drop items, or knock things over.

  Proprioceptive input comprises sensory input to activate the joints and muscles so they become more responsive. Pushing or pulling things, crawling, and ball exercises can help improve muscle tone, coordination, and calming of the brain (Lumiere Children's Therapy 2017).

- **Deep-Pressure Tactile Input:** People with Autism who have proprioceptive difficulties may need physical contact, which can make them enjoy being bear-hugged but can also make them do things like crash into walls and other surfaces. Deep-pressure tactile input can help by calming them and reducing anxiety while also improving their sense of body awareness.

  Dr. Temple Grandin has written a paper about a "squeeze machine" she created when she turned eighteen. This machine, she says, helped her calm down her anxiety and panic attacks, especially when she would use it twice a day for fifteen minutes each session. The device delivered a deep touch pressure, which has been found in various studies to help children with Autism and sensory processing disorders (Bestbier and Williams 2017).

Through deep-pressure tactile input, proprioceptive input can be delivered via firm stroking, hugging, squeezing, compression, or swaddling. Today, many OTs employ some of Grandin's theories and techniques (Otsimo 2023).

Obtaining the help of an OT is highly recommended, not only because this professional can help your child with their specific sensory challenges but also because the information they provide is vital to share with your child's teachers. By knowing your child's triggers and key strategies for helping them calm down, her teachers can craft a more positive and fruitful learning experience for her.

LETTING TEACHERS KNOW ABOUT YOUR CHILD'S SENSORY CHALLENGES

When your child starts a new school year, I suggest making an appointment as early as possible with her teachers so you can share challenges and strategies. Present teachers with a report provided by her occupational therapist and share your own observations. Even if you present an OT-written report, you will most likely have plenty of additional information to contribute, including specific sensitivities to sounds, touch, or visual stimuli. Let them know if your child has meltdowns or if loud noises (for instance, school assemblies or fire drills) are a trigger for her (Morin, n.d.).

If your child has an IEP or 504 Plan, bring a copy for her teachers and ask them to read it. Let them know about any equipment she may need, including fidget items, cushions, or headphones. Inform them of her interests and strengths, too, and let them know if and how you have used these interests to teach other topics. Don't hesitate to ask for the teachers' opinions. They may have taught Autistic students in the past or know of strategies they can try out with your child.

Finally, ask them how you can help. Let them know from the start that you are keen to work as a team with them and that you are open to any observations or suggestions. Establish how you wish to stay in touch and ask them to let you know of any challenges before they become too big to manage.

As a parent, you know the main strategies that work for your child. I thought it might be helpful to share just a few testimonies revealing accommodations that parents of some of my students and friends have asked teachers to accommodate:

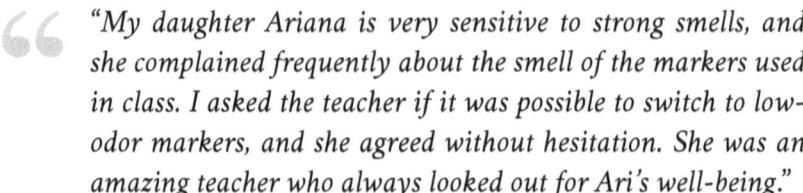

> *"My daughter Ariana is very sensitive to strong smells, and she complained frequently about the smell of the markers used in class. I asked the teacher if it was possible to switch to low-odor markers, and she agreed without hesitation. She was an amazing teacher who always looked out for Ari's well-being."*
>
> — STEPHANIE, 42

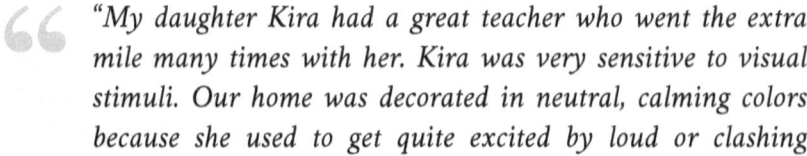

> *"Marina does not handle transitions well. When I would drop her at school, she would cry because she did not want to enter the classroom. She would also have a meltdown if she was taking part in an activity and the teacher ended it abruptly. I began taking her to school around fifteen minutes early. It gave us time to bond before she started. I also asked the teacher to let her know that an activity was about to end at least ten minutes before so she could wrap her head around the transition."*
>
> — MIGUEL, 35

> *"My daughter Kira had a great teacher who went the extra mile many times with her. Kira was very sensitive to visual stimuli. Our home was decorated in neutral, calming colors because she used to get quite excited by loud or clashing*

colors. When she was eight and she started fourth grade, I was stunned by the classroom decor. I knew from the start she would react to it, and I was right. The classroom had loads of loud primary colors, artwork, and patterns. I kept quiet at first, but when the teacher told me Kira had had more than one meltdown in a few days, I asked the teacher if it would be possible to take down some of the decor. She did that very day and it made a difference for Kira. I am so appreciative to teachers like her who always put children first."

— CLAUDIA, 51

"One of the best things I did was to talk to my daughter Cora's teacher about finding her a quiet space where she could have a little 'me time' and calm down. Cora felt overwhelmed by having to be in the company of others all the time, and having a place where she could be with herself and practice a bit of breathing really helped."

— ADARA, 54

Below are more strategies I have used myself in class (and a few suggested by my colleagues):

- Give children a footstool so their feet have a solid base upon which to rest.
- Let them complete their work while lying on the floor.
- Seat them away from doors or windows so they won't be distracted by what is going on outside.
- Let them sit on an exercise ball instead of a chair.
- Let them use sensory tools recommended by their OT, such as bouncy chairs, weighted vests, or earplugs.
- Allowing them to chew gum in class.
- Let them walk around the classroom while they were learning something new.

- Warn them when a loud noise was about to start.
- Teach them to ask for breaks when they are feeling a little stressed out or need to move.

Encourage your child to employ the strategies that work for her at school (Laurie 2022). For instance, if she feels overwhelmed when other kids bump into her, tell her that it's okay to ask her teacher if she can stand at the front or back of a line so she has more space to herself. She may also find it useful to snack on chewy or crunchy snacks for recess or bring a small bottle of essential oil or a favorite toy to school.

CALMING EXERCISES AND ACTIVITIES

Share exercises your child can use when sensory overload arises, letting her preferences lead the way. Just a few that may resonate with her include:

Breathing Exercises

In my first book, I shared many breathing exercises with you, but here are a few more you might like to try out:

- **Balloon Breathing:** Ask your child to close her eyes and imagine her lungs as a balloon. Next, ask her to inhale slowly and visualize the balloon inflating. Then, ask her to exhale gently, picturing her internal balloon deflating. Finally, invite her to focus on her breath and the balloon's expansion and contraction for a few minutes.
- **Stuffed Animal Breathing:** Ask your child to lie on her back. Place a favorite stuffed animal on her belly. Instruct her to breathe deeply enough to make the stuffed animal rise. Ask her to watch the stuffed animal fall as she exhales. Recommend that she repeat this exercise for a few minutes. If you wish, play soft background music to enhance calmness.

- **Dragon Breath Counting:** Invite your child to stand or sit comfortably. Tell her to imagine she is a friendly dragon. Ask her to inhale deeply through the nose, then exhale slowly while counting out loud: "One … Two … Three … Four …" Challenge her to make her dragon breathe longer each time. Invite her to use hand motions to mimic a dragon's wings expanding and contracting. Repeat the exercise three to five times.

Proprioceptive Exercises

These exercises work by providing calming input to the body. They can involve pressure and movement involving the muscles and joints. Just a few exercises that may help your child reduce the impact of sensory overload include (Centre for Autism Middletown, n.d.):

- Pushing up against a wall with her hands or back to create resistance

- Exercises engaging the large muscles such as animal walks (crab-walking, bear crawling, frog jumps) or carrying heavy objects

- Pushing or pulling activities, such as pushing a wagon filled with soft toys

- Jumping and climbing activities like trampoline jumping, jumping onto a soft pile of pillows or bean bags, or making her way through a backyard obstacle course

- Resistance and squeezing activities like squeezing a stress ball, using a weighted blanket, or pressing her palms together and holding it for a few seconds

- Oral motor activities like sipping through a straw or chewing crunchy foods

Visual and Auditory Distraction Techniques

Visual and auditory input can help distract a child from overwhelming stimuli. For instance, your child may enjoy watching a video with images of nature, listening to calming music, or sitting in a room with soft lighting (Special Strong, n.d.). Some parents I've met use nature sounds or white noise to give their children auditory comfort. In my first book, *Raising an Autistic Girl: Modern ASD Strategies for Successful Parenting*, I provided many calming activities, one of which was creating a glitter jar. I could personally stare at glitter settling in a jar for countless minutes! I find it very calming. When I was a child, I had a lava lamp that enthralled me!

Yoga

Several studies have shown yoga to be beneficial to kids with ASD. In particular, this ancient practice has been proven to help improve verbal and nonverbal communication skills, social skills such as empathy and teamwork, attention, emotional self-regulation, physiological and psychological balance, motor skills, and sensory integration (Bhavanani 2019).

Yoga poses you may enjoy teaching your child include:

- **The Child's Pose:** Ask your child to kneel on the floor, sit back on her heels, stretch her arms forward on the ground, and rest her forehead on the floor.

- **The Cat-Cow Stretch:** Invite your child to get on all fours and round her back, tuck her chin to her chest, and pull her belly in (like a cat). Next, tell her to arch her back, lift her head and tailbone toward the ceiling, and let her belly drop (like a cow). Invite her to slowly transition between these two poses a few times.

- **Butterfly Pose:** Ask your child to sit on the floor, bring the soles of her feet together, and let her knees drop to the sides. Ask her to hold her feet with her hands and try to feel a gentle stretch in her hips and inner thighs.

Grounding Exercise

This exercise aims to help your child bring her mind to "the here and now" (Calm, n.d.). To commence, simply invite her to take part in a scavenger hunt. Next, ask her to find five things she can see, four things she can touch, three things she can hear, two things she can smell, and one thing she can taste.

SENSORY-FRIENDLY WEBSITES AND APPS:

One of the ways I enjoy soothing myself when I experience sensory overload is by taking a drive by myself and listening to loud music. When I'm in the mood for something quieter, I use an app called Breathe, which guides me through a deep breathing session that calms down my anxiety and brings my heart rate down. The app has an animation that grows with each inhalation and shrinks with each exhalation. You can change the duration of your breathing session from one to five minutes and set a breath rate from four breaths per minute to ten breaths per minute. Your child may enjoy watching the animation and allowing it to guide her breathing rate, too.

Another app that many parents rave about is Dreamy Kid, a meditation app that has everyday meditations for different parts of the day, including starting the day and falling asleep. The app also has positive affirmations that kids can repeat to themselves to encourage positive thinking, sleep stories, and guided journeys to places that invoke feelings of relaxation, empowerment, or calm. It also allows users to focus on specific issues such as anxiety and anger management and has "healing activities" that encourage children to work with sound, breath, and movement to encourage dynamic equilibrium in the body's systems.

A third app many parents recommend is Calm Kids, which is centered on meditation and sleep. It has mindfulness meditation programs, sleep stories, lullabies, soundscapes, and much more. One of the best things about this app is that it is constantly being updated. For instance, new bedtime stories are released two to three times a month. The narrators are great, too. They include actors like Maya Rudolph, Wanda Sykes, and Diane Keaton.

End-of-Chapter Activity: Make a Sensory Tool Kit

A sensory tool kit is a collection of items you can assemble alongside your child to keep her calm and grounded at school. I suggest that the tool kit should have at least five items and that each item should appeal to one of her five senses (sight, touch, sound, taste, and smell). To create your kit, follow these steps (LifeSpring Counseling Services, n.d.):

1. Invite your child to choose one visually grounding item. It could be a picture of her pet, a small toy she loves, a small glitter jar or snow globe, a nature scene, a mandala she has colored, or a positive affirmation card with encouraging messages and drawings.
2. Now, ask her to select one item that grounds her through sound. It could be a recording of her pet dog snoring while it sleeps, a cat purring, or a nature sound. She can keep this recording on her phone or another small device she takes to school.
3. Ask her to gather an item that grounds her through the sense of touch. It could be a stress ball, worry beads, or a fuzzy piece of fabric.
4. Invite her to select an item that grounds her through her sense of smell. It could be a small bottle of perfume or essential oil, a scented candle, or a piece of scented stationery.
5. Ask her to gather an item that grounds her through her sense of taste. This could be a stick of gum, hard candy, or something crunchy.

Now put all these items into a small envelope, Ziploc bag, or box. Encourage her to open the box and engage with these items when she wishes to calm her senses.

In this chapter, we have covered sensory challenges, which can be one of the toughest obstacles kids face at school. A typical school day can be long, and a child may not have the calming environment you have created for her at home. You have seen how forming a bond with your child's teacher and arming your child with self-soothing tools can be a big help. In the next chapter, we will turn to another important goal: helping your child make meaningful friendships.

HELP AUTISTIC GIRLS REALIZE THEIR WORTH

"Behind every young child who believes in himself is a parent who believed first."

— MATTHEW L. JACOBSON

Congratulations on making it halfway through this book. I hope you are inspired to try the many strategies I have shared to make your child's school years more fulfilling. You have seen that the first step in doing so is knowing more about Autism—how it impacts your child's learning, sensory development, and social interaction. Knowing how the Autistic brain works gives you vital information you can share with teachers and your child's team of professionals so they can personalize learning and therapeutic approaches.

At the very start of this book, I mentioned the link between the way others treat your child and their self-esteem. When a child is constantly berated, told to do things differently, or forced to behave the way everyone else does, it sends them a negative message. By now, you have seen that the strategies I suggest do all the opposite. They encourage your child to tap into her strengths, create her routines and schedules alongside you, and soothe her senses in the ways that feel right for her.

As an Autistic woman, I can vouch for the confidence that arises when you allow a girl to feel valued as she is, irrespective of how different her interests and behaviors may be from those of neurotypical children. I wrote this book to reach as many parents of Autistic girls as possible so they can start effecting the kind of change that will help their daughter live fully, authentically, and meaningfully. I hope you can help me achieve this goal by sharing your opinion with other parents.

By leaving a review of this book on Amazon, you'll show other parents where they can find a guide that advocates for Autistic girls' rights to be understood, valued, and cherished.

Thanks for your support. In the next half of the book, you will find more techniques for creating a positive environment for your child. In Chapter 6, we will dive right into the important topic of making and sustaining true friendships.

Scan the QR code below to leave your review:

S: SEEKING CONNECTION

> *"Every person has some weakness or some limitation, but our limitations are a good thing because they make us an expert in other areas or areas that we're stronger in. As we use our strengths, we compensate for our weaknesses."*
>
> — RON SANDISON (ELS FOR AUTISM 2023)

Ron Sandison's view on the value of sharing exactly who you are, warts and all, really strikes a chord with me because I spent my school years doing exactly the opposite. There was a lot of bullying taking place at school, and in order to survive, I felt I had to fit in … and that meant masking the behaviors that could lead others to mark me as "different." Masking made my day-to-day life run seemingly smoother, but I realized that I had given up too much (my peace of mind, my need to stim, and my deep wish for connection) to make life easier. And as a whole, the tension of masking outweighed its benefits.

I am fascinated by the writings of Brené Brown, the academic, author, and podcaster who has done so much to change the way people see vulnerability. She states that when she was younger, she always sought to mask her vulnerability. However, through her research, she came to one important conclusion: authentic connection is born out of vulnerability, not of strength. She states, "Vulnerability is courage. It's about the willingness to show up and be seen in our lives. And in those moments when we show up, I think those are the most powerful, meaning-making moments of our lives, even if they don't go well. I think they define who we are" (Tippett 2015).

So what exactly does "showing up" mean for an Autistic girl? Well, it could mean bringing a fidget tool to school and giving an honest answer about why she needs it when asked. It could involve telling her friend she needs some quiet time because her senses are overloaded, or sharing the fact that she is Autistic and needs to move while she learns.

For many Autistic girls and women, the courage to be vulnerable takes time, and I am living proof of that. When you are honest and vulnerable about your needs, you risk being judged, criticized, or shamed by others. Yet people may criticize or judge you even if you mask, so there's not much to be gained in appearing to be someone you're not. In this chapter, I hope to demonstrate why encouraging your child to be herself is one of the best gifts you can give her. Even when your daughter tries and "fails" at something, you can help her feel good about having made an effort and allow her to express her disappointment freely.

Say she opens up to someone about a sensory need, and the person calls her a name. You can tell her something like, "I'm so proud of you not only for trying but also for letting us know how much you wanted to be accepted ... it takes a brave person to do that."

Finding a balance between trying to fit in (which is universal for kids) and being one's authentic self (which delivers a unique sense of freedom and relief) can be tough. Your child can lead the way when it comes to vulnerability. She certainly should not be forced to reveal more than she is comfortable with. However, at least in your own home and with your family and close friends, she should know that her vulnerability is respected, accepted, and celebrated. In time, she will hopefully discover that the friends who love her for who she is, those who do not shame her for being herself, are those who are worth keeping by her side. Devon Price called them "strawberry people"—those who never require you to mask your authentic self (Price 2022).

SOCIAL CHALLENGES FACED BY AUTISTIC GIRLS

There are many social challenges that make it harder for Autistic girls to forge friendships. I have mentioned how sensory challenges can make it harder for us to pay attention when we are hyper-reactive or hypo-reactive to sensory input. In addition, we have difficulty reading social cues such as body language and facial expressions, sarcasm and figurative language, subtle social signs, social etiquette, and emotional states. We may struggle to take turns in conversations and be confused about how much personal space we need to give others. Our intense interests can also be perplexing to others. When we are into something, we can talk about it endlessly and annoy those who aren't interested in the same topic (Sturrock et al. 2021).

My Autistic friends and I often say that even when we have formed part of relatively large friend groups, we've always had the sensation that we were merely surviving, not creating close bonds. We also share difficulties in understanding when someone is being serious because we tend to take things literally.

The unspoken rules that governed girl groups at school were often way too complex for our understanding when we were younger. Moreover, white lies, gossip, judgments, and relational bullying would often go over our heads. Also known as social bullying, these actions are non-physical aggressions that aim to harm someone's relationships, social status, or reputation. They are subtle and harder to detect than physical aggression, but they leave deep wounds that can take years (and therapy) to overcome.

All these reasons explain why many Autistic people often feel more comfortable in the company of Autistic friends. One study shows that Autistic people tend to find interactions with other Autistic people less tiring, less stressful, simpler, more familiar in terms of communication styles, and easier to understand (Crompton et al. 2020). Interestingly, studies have shown that Autistic and non-Autistic kids have trouble understanding each other's thoughts, emotions, wants, and needs. They also rate their mutual friendship as being lower in closeness, security-intimacy, and the provision of help (O'Connor et al. 2022).

When we are with other Autistic people, we often feel a greater sense of belonging and understanding (Meyer 2024a). This is why it can be very useful to join support groups and meet up with other parents of Autistic kids. Almost all states and cities have local support groups, and a quick online search will show you where your closest group is.

When speaking with my close friends who are Autistic, we often talk about how hard it can be to fulfill social expectations. For instance, if a neighbor needs help moving and says something like, "Oh no, I have so much packing to do this weekend. I don't know how I'll get it all done," we might answer, "That sounds tough," and not offer to help, simply because our friend has not explicitly asked for help.

Research shows that neurotypical women typically maintain larger friend groups, while Autistic women often prefer fewer, closer, and more intense friendships. Some of these friendships can become their "special interest" (Pellicano and Sedgewick 2017). While in my childhood I formed part of a large group of friends at school, I no longer feel the same need to be accepted by, say, the group of moms at my children's school or other larger groups. I have a small group of friends with whom I share interests or whom I have known for years and who I know accept me as I am. I simply don't have the energy to waste on relationships that don't feel mutual, and I am quite unapologetic about that.

SOCIAL ANXIETY IN AUTISTIC GIRLS

Around 72 percent of children with Autism have at least one psychiatric disorder (such as depression or anxiety). In particular, difficulties with social motivation and communication are linked to social anxiety or social phobia (Briot et al. 2020). Social anxiety causes kids to fear being judged by others, which can lead to an avoidance of social situations as a whole (Spain et al. 2018). It can also cause them to keep their interactions with others brief and superficial, which can damage friendships over time. Your child may desperately want to make friends but fear other kids' motivations. Because Autistic individuals tend to interpret words literally, they may assume other people have good intentions and feel very hurt and disappointed when they discover otherwise (Pellicano and Sedgewick 2017).

Social anxiety takes time and patience to manage. Showing your child how to self-soothe and rely on her sensory tool kit can help, as can giving her many opportunities to interact with others at her own pace.

"I went to a school that specialized in Autism. My parents moved me there when I was ten and life got a lot better compared to how it was in my old school. For one, I was allowed to bring my stress ball and fidget toys. The teacher also allowed me to answer questions while pacing to and from the blackboard. Moving helped me memorize what I was learning and tell others about it. I also have social anxiety, but it got a lot better when I moved from my old school to my new one."

— KRISTA, 29

ALEXITHYMIA AND AUTISM

Alexithymia is a personality trait characterized by difficulties with recognizing, identifying, and describing feelings or emotions (Hogeveen and Grafman 2021). Alexithymia and Autism overlap at high rates, with an estimated 50–60 percent of Autistic people having alexithymia. The co-occurrence of Autism and alexithymia has led to diagnostic confusion and perpetuated unuseful stereotypes about Autistic people. Many of the false assumptions about Autistic people (for instance, that we struggle with empathy, reciprocity, and identifying our feelings) can, in fact, be attributed to alexithymia (Neff, n.d.). Indeed, scientists have found that alexithymia is linked to lower empathy and social isolation (Silvertant 2020). For instance, people with alexithymia can have difficulty in identifying facial expressions. They may, therefore, fail to pick up signs that someone is sad, angry, or not interested in interacting with others.

People who have both alexithymia and Autism can have higher rates of relationship struggles, depression, and anxiety. They may also find emotional regulation challenging and struggle with interoception—the sense that allows you to answer the question "How do I feel?" at any given moment. For instance, it allows you to identify when your heart is beating fast, you are feeling hot or cold, your muscles are tense, or you're hungry or thirsty (Barker et al. 2021).

In one relatively recent study (Weiner et al. 2023), scientists found that Autistic girls can find emotional regulation tougher than boys. In the study, they scored higher for emotional reactivity than boys of all ages (from age four to twenty) and scored higher for depressed mood. Neurotypical girls and boys had a similar gap.

Emotional regulation (the ability to effectively manage one's emotions) is a vital skill for making and sustaining friendships because it empowers us to accept things as they are, positively reframe thoughts and situations, refocus on what is important, and put things in perspective. This is in contrast to maladaptive reactions such as ruminating over conflicts, catastrophizing situations, and blaming oneself or others (Ricciardi et al. 2022).

Even though alexithymia isn't officially recognized in the DSM-5, it can be diagnosed by a mental health professional. There is no single test for it, and it may take time to obtain a diagnosis, but if the professional believes your child has alexithymia, they may recommend approaches such as cognitive-behavioral therapy (CBT) (Cherney 2024). This therapy can help your child recognize, manage, and express emotions that may not be obvious to them. The therapist may utilize cognitive reappraisal techniques to alter the way your child views a situation and help her understand that a given stimulus is not necessarily aimed at causing her harm (Deolinda 2025). You can also try using supports such as images of people displaying different emotions to enhance her ability to recognize facial expressions. I also recommend taking part in role-plays so your child can practice demonstrating those emotions.

FRIENDSHIP PREFERENCES FOR AUTISTIC GIRLS

In chapter 1, I mentioned that Autistic girls sometimes have just one or two close friends. It is not that they don't desire to form relationships with others or that they don't have empathy. Instead, their difficulties with social interaction and communication and restricted or repetitive behaviors, interests, and activities are often not accepted by neurotypical peers. Research shows that Autistic children, both in middle childhood and adolescence, tend to have fewer friends than non-Autistic peers.

As a whole, although Autistic girls are more socially motivated than Autistic boys and appear to "fit in" with their peers more, they may have difficulty recognizing reciprocal friendship. For instance, the friendships they report are less likely to be reciprocated by their nominated friend than is the case for non-Autistic kids (Libster et al. 2023).

Some Autistic girls seem socially extroverted but find it hard to bond with others. Statistics have also shown that they can be treated unkindly, even within their "friendship groups" (Rowley et al. 2012). As they grow into adolescence, they develop a more complex understanding of friendship and may begin redefining their friendships and feeling a greater sense of loneliness. There are some notable similarities between boys and girls. Both genders report having at least one friend, though in adolescence, some report having no friends or being uncertain whether they have friends. However, although both genders are equally likely to report feeling lonely at times, several Autistic boys and girls say they are frequently lonely.

There are also key differences. For instance, while girls are more likely to refer to personality when defining friendship, boys usually refer more to shared interests with their friends (Libster et al. 2023). Both Autistic and neurotypical friendships seek emotional closeness, yet boys tend to place a greater value on shared interests and activities. Additionally, research comparing Autistic girls' social skills to those of neurotypical girls and Autistic boys shows that Autistic girls' social interaction tends to be more conversation-based, while that of Autistic boys tends to be more play- or activity-based.

Autistic girls are less likely to play alone than boys, which contrasts with the stereotype of Autistic people preferring solitary activities. It also partially explains why Autistic girls tend to be diagnosed later than boys (Misheva 2024).

Autistic girls tend to have more narrow social networks than neurotypical girls, and their friendships are more intense, with studies showing that individual best friends often become the main focus of their social lives (Sedgewick et al. 2019). Having just one close friend may be more manageable than having to deal with the changing dynamics of multiple relationships. Try to imagine that all of us have a "friendship battery." Autistic girls may only have enough energy in their battery for one friendship rather than multiple. Research has also shown that when conflicts with friends arise, Autistic girls tend to assume that they are at fault and may jump to the conclusion that the friendship cannot be fixed. They may, therefore, withdraw from friends who still wish to have them in their lives (Sedgewick et al. 2018). Losing friends can be highly distressing for a child who only has one or two close friends. It can harm their mental health and influence their ability to attend school—for instance, if their friend suddenly spends more time with other kids or moves to a new school.

Psychologist and author Dr. Emilia Misheva reports that in her practice, she has heard distressed Autistic girls being referred to as "controlling," "domineering," or "manipulative" because they wanted to have just one close friend (Misheva 2024). She reminds readers that it is not a matter of control or dominance but rather a wish to have their emotional needs met. She laments the fact that Autistic girls are often blamed without the *causes* for their behavior being taken into account. For instance, if an Autistic girl becomes upset when her best friend wants to play with other children, attributing malicious intent to her reaction is simplistic because it fails to take into account why she feels this way. For instance, her internal battery may simply not be large enough to allow her to play with many kids at once. She may find conversations too hard to follow, other kids may not be as patient as her best friends, or she may find the sensory input too much to bear. Similarly, a girl may be judged if she steers the topic of the conversation to her special interests. Doing so is not selfish; it is her way of talking about something she feels confident about. It reduces unpredictability and the anxiety associated with it.

Sarah Hendrickx notes that many Autistic girls and women identify themselves as "tomboys" and that they may find girls to be more complex and nuanced in their social skills than boys. This is particularly true in adolescence when friendships tend to shift their focus from shared interests to personalities. They may have difficulty understanding girl group dynamics and feel inadequate when interacting with others. Autistic girls may also shun typical "girls' toys" and enjoy playing more with traditional "boys' toys" (Hendrickx 2015).

You have a powerful role to play in helping your child accept that there is nothing wrong with, for instance, preferring to have one or two friends instead of forming part of a big group. You can model acceptance, share her special interests, and help explain so-called domineering behaviors to others, including the parents of her good friends. You can gently provide your daughter with numerous opportunities to meet new people and perhaps click strongly with one or more friends inside or outside their school setting. As adults, I believe the most beneficial role we can take is that of a facilitator. We gain more by providing our children with chances to meet others than by forcing them to form part of big groups of children they do not connect with.

The good news is that it does get better with time. My Autistic friends and I often talk about how we have become far more self-aware over the years. Many of us are more than happy to have one or two friends, and we no longer feel like we have to change to fit in. Today, I know it is okay to have a smaller group of friends, be alone sometimes, or just be with my wife.

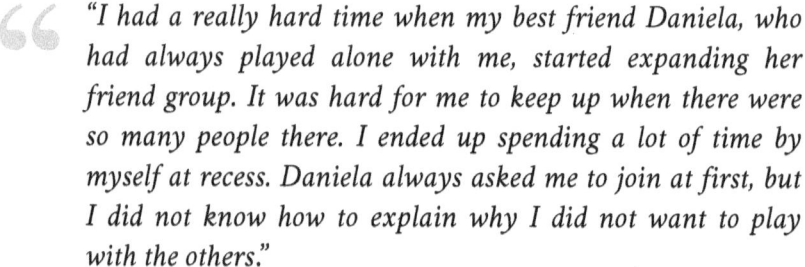

"I had a really hard time when my best friend Daniela, who had always played alone with me, started expanding her friend group. It was hard for me to keep up when there were so many people there. I ended up spending a lot of time by myself at recess. Daniela always asked me to join at first, but I did not know how to explain why I did not want to play with the others."

— WILLA, 21

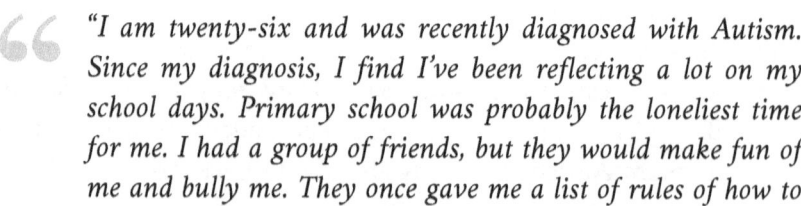

"I am twenty-six and was recently diagnosed with Autism. Since my diagnosis, I find I've been reflecting a lot on my school days. Primary school was probably the loneliest time for me. I had a group of friends, but they would make fun of me and bully me. They once gave me a list of rules of how to behave that they had written with their parents! In my adolescence, I began hanging out more with boys, particularly neurodivergent boys. They made me feel more accepted, though they would sometimes exclude me from their online gaming groups. As an adult, I still find it easier to talk to men, but I do have a couple of close friends who are women. I find that they have stuck with me through thick and thin and are always there to listen when I'm having a bad day."

— VICKY, 26

"I have a lot of unresolved trauma from primary and middle school because the girls I was 'friends' with constantly belittled and betrayed me. The boys weren't little angels either, but they seemed more upfront when they had conflicts with me. They would tell me directly what they didn't like instead of gossiping and segregating me. I found that there is often a big power imbalance in toxic girl groups."

— AUGIE, 23

HELPING YOUR DAUGHTER FIND HER STRAWBERRY PEOPLE

I'd love to get back to Devon Price's idea of the importance of helping your child find her strawberry people—those who love and accept her unconditionally. He traces this term to writer Samuel Dylan Finch, who writes that he used to push away people who were loving and available to him because he associated loving others with having to work hard to keep them happy (people-pleasing). This led him to many unhealthy relationships involving abuse and exploitation, both personally and professionally. In time, he realized he needed to "rewire his brain's social pathways" and make a list of people who were worthy of his friendship. He thus made a list of people who were very loving and put strawberry emojis by their names in his phone contact list. They became his "strawberry people"—the tried-and-tested, unconditional friends who helped him think or grow (Price 2022).

This quote by Autistic self-connection coach and shadow worker Sadie Tichelaar sums up the importance of finding real friends: "The whole idea of having friendships is to have connections and to be seen and to feel valued and reciprocate those connections. Yet the whole time, we're ... valuing 'I need to act a certain way to fit in,' rather than, 'How can I be myself and find the people that I can belong with because we'll all be having an allowance for everyone being their slightly weird, awkward, wonderful, messy selves'" (Alex Alexander 2023).

As a parent, you can help your child make her list of strawberry people. The list does not have to have more than one or two people. Use the checklist at the end of this chapter if you wish.

HELPING YOUR CHILD FIND SPECIAL INTEREST GROUPS

School is not the only place where your child can meet people and establish meaningful bonds. I mentioned that it can also be helpful for them to join special interest groups and meet up with other Autistic children. There will undoubtedly be many local groups you can find through your connections on social media and other online platforms. Just a few platforms helping kids connect include:

- **Autistic Girls Network:** This UK-based organization features face-to-face groups for girls and nonbinary people aged nine to twenty-five (Autistic Girls Network, n.d.).
- **Friend in Me:** A social group connecting kids with disabilities and neurotypical student volunteers through free, fun online games and conversations via Zoom on a one-to-one basis every week (Friend in Me, n.d.).
- **The Autism Project (TAP):** This organization offers social skills groups led by speech-language pathologists,

occupational therapists, mental health practitioners, and other professionals for ages 5–10, pre-teens, teens, and young adults (The Autism Project, n.d.). Note that some Autistic people and advocates feel that social skills training encourages masking because it includes activities such as scripting. However, others do find some help with social skills to be useful—for instance, for aiding in self-advocacy, independence, and communication. Social skills groups may encourage kids to learn "scripts" they can use specific situations, such as breaking the ice at a party or speaking on the phone. Each child and family need to make their own decisions with respect to whether this approach is for them.

SIBLINGS AS A SOURCE OF SUPPORT AND FRIENDSHIP FOR AUTISTIC KIDS

If your child has siblings, they can play an important role in helping her feel loved and cherished. They can be a source of comfort, companionship, and understanding, which can positively impact their siblings' social skills and overall growth and development. They can also be powerful Autism advocates, helping others understand what Autism is, challenging myths and misconceptions, and promoting acceptance (Apex ABA Therapy 2024b).

You can foster this unique bond between your children by seeking professional support and guidance. Many of my friends who are parents of Autistic children encourage their neurotypical kids to sign up for sibling support groups and programs. Doing so helps them deal with both the challenges and rewards of having an Autistic brother or sister. As much as your kids love their sibling, they may have challenging feelings they need to know how to manage. For instance, they may be jealous about the amount of time you spend with her. They may also feel discouraged if she does not want to play. Some may feel embarrassed by unwanted attention that can arise during family outings. Support groups can help them understand that their feelings are natural and that they are not alone (Raising Children, n.d.-a).

You can also do plenty at home to boost your children's awareness of Autism. You can provide age-appropriate resources, such as books and videos that give them insight into the way their sibling thinks and feels. It also helps to create an open environment at home, one in which kids can freely ask questions and express their emotions. If neurotypical siblings are having a rough time or feel a bit confused about their Autistic sibling's behavior or experiences, listen to them actively. That means giving them your full attention, reflecting on what they have said, asking pertinent questions, and avoiding the urge to interrupt or give unsolicited advice. Acknowledge their difficult feelings and let them know there's nothing wrong with feeling a bit confused or frustrated. Try to make special (one-on-one) time for all your children so they all feel special and loved. Set fair rules and responsibilities where possible. For instance, you can find tasks and chores that suit your children's respective ages, strengths, and stages of development. Be consistent in how you handle aggressive or hurtful behavior from all your children.

Finally, do your best to seek out experiences that all your kids can enjoy together. Encourage your kids to delve a bit into interests and activities their Autistic sibling enjoys, and help them communicate in the way she best understands. I mentioned earlier that Autistic people can have difficulty understanding sarcasm or irony. Therefore, you can teach siblings how to use precise, clear, concise language. You can also model patience and point out nonverbal cues that may show their Autistic sibling is overwhelmed and needs a break. Many parents also find it helpful to include siblings in the creation of visual supports (like schedules or social stories) so that they understand the importance of routines for people with Autism.

End-of-Chapter Activity: Strawberry People Checklist

Use the following checklist to help your child find loving, supportive friends (Price 2022). Once they make their list, create a poster and stick strawberry stickers next to the names. Revise the list every few weeks, as your child may want to add or remove names.

You don't have to use all the questions. I recommend choosing three to five.

1. Who makes you happy to be around them?
2. Who listens to you when you are talking about the things you like?
3. Who invites you to play or join in activities?
4. Who doesn't mind if you need some quiet time?
5. Who accepts your interests and hobbies?
6. Who helps you when you are feeling overwhelmed?
7. Who doesn't make fun of you ever?
8. Who stands up for you when others are unkind?
9. Who celebrates your achievements, big or small?
10. Who is patient with you when you are learning things?
11. Who remembers important things about you, like your favorite foods or colors?

In this chapter, we have focused on helping your child make and sustain friendships. You have seen how it helps to allow your child to define their friendship needs and to help them appreciate friends who love them just as they are. In the next chapter, we will move to technological matters, discussing top tech tools that can help your child with learning, sensory, and communication challenges.

H: HARNESSING SMART TECHNOLOGY

> *"Assistive technology (AT) tools provide personalized technological solutions for people with Autism, helping them overcome communication barriers and adapting to their specific needs. These tools amplify skills and improve independence, significantly contributing to the quality of life of people with Autism"*
>
> — (IANNONE AND GIANSANTI 2023).

New advances in technology have opened many avenues for people with Autism, providing them with innovative tools to learn, communicate, and manage their daily lives with greater ease. In this chapter, I will share a few websites, apps, and tools that many parents of Autistic children find useful. However, before discussing specific apps and products, know that it may take you a bit of trial and error before you find the technologies that make a positive difference to your child at home, at school, and in social settings. Autism is a spectrum encompassing a wide range of ages, symptoms, and needs, meaning no single device, app, or system will suit everyone. Second, tech advances at breakneck speed, which can make it hard for physicians, therapists, and parents to keep up with everything that's out. Finally, some technology that may be extremely useful to your child may not be tagged as "for Autism." For all these reasons, being active in the Autism community and sharing information with professionals, friends, and fellow parents is vital.

When looking through this list, don't forget the tools for creating routines that I suggested in Chapter 3. They can also form part of your child's arsenal to stay on top of their goals.

TECH FOR LEARNING

The following apps can help your kids with their learning objectives (helloEd 2023):

Gemiini: This program provides 100 percent web-based, on-demand therapy through research-based modeling for learners. It can be used by kids, parents, therapists, and schools and is available worldwide. It comprises video therapy and teaching tools that teach new information and train or retrain the brain to think. The videos break down information into small bites to teach speech, reading, language, social, and life skills. Each video focuses on one concept, and the program has a huge library of content that is constantly being added to and updated.

Kids can access the videos while they're in the car, at a park, or at home. The videos use repetition, audio-visual pairing, and context to boost retention. Each concept is presented as an independent learning bite. The learner is exposed repeatedly to a word in three different contexts: a name card (the actor says the word in front of a title card with the word name and a picture of the word), mouth view (featuring the actor's mouth up-close as they say the word), and action scene (this could feature actor vignettes, animations, or other general contexts) to show how a word is used in daily life. For further information, see www.gemiini.org

Tiimo Visual Daily Planner: Tiimo is an app that allows users of all ages to plan their daily lives and achieve their goals thanks to customizable, playful, highly visual features. It can be accessed via a smartphone or smartwatch that supports executive function challenges. You can use it to create your own visual schedule, and the app will remind you of it throughout the day and give you a little nudge when activities are starting or ending. You can add an icon and checklist to each activity to celebrate every task achieved. For further information, see www.tiimoapp.com

Goally: In chapter 3, I mentioned one of Goally's most popular apps: CoPilot, which can help kids create customized schedules. Goally actually offers numerous apps that can help kids create and follow routines and boost their productivity and independence. You can use these apps on a smartphone or Goally's distraction-free device. Features to watch out for include digital token boards for rewards and behavior management, visual timers for activities, behavior tracking, and team access to data for optimal coordination. For further information, see www.getgoally.com

TECH FOR COMMUNICATION

The following apps, devices, and companies can help your child communicate with others (helloEd 2023):

Tobii Dynavox: Tobii Dynavox is a leading assistive communication organization that creates custom-designed communication aids and offers a support system to enable people with Autism and other disabilities to communicate and live their best lives. The company has many products and assistive services, including speech-generating devices, eye trackers, and communication/access apps. In order to obtain a device, your child will need an initial evaluation. They will then receive a recommendation for an Augmentative and Alternative Communication (AAC) device and receive assistance in obtaining funding for it and setting it up. You and your child will also receive ongoing support to ensure you are getting the most out of your device and help you adapt the device to your child's needs. For further information, see www.us.tobiidynavox.com

Proloquo2Go app: This award-winning AAC app enables non-speaking children and adults to express themselves confidently and initiate conversations. It is available in four languages (English, Spanish, French, and Dutch) and contains over 27,000 symbols that users can use to communicate effectively. It supports the development of vocabulary and language skills, helping users move from single words to complex sentences and allowing you to customize words and looks to match your child's preferred style. You can also add photos of your family and friends to buttons if you wish. For further information, see www.assistiveware.com

GoTalk: Attainment (the company that produces GoTalk) boasts over twenty-five years in the AAC industry, and it has a wide range of AAC devices and apps that enable users to communicate their wants and needs. Users can create their own communication templates, incorporating different buttons to each screen. Any text you add to the buttons is read aloud by the device. You can also add your own voice as the label for each button for a more familiar feel. For further information, see www.attainmentcompany.com

AbleNet: AbleNet has a wide range of assistive technology devices for learning and communication, including AAC devices, switches, and support devices for computer and table access. It provides product support, helping your child get started with the device or speech app. For further information, see www.ablenetinc.com

CommBoards AAC: This is a Picture Exchange Communication System (PECS) app, which was born as a project meant to help the developers' close friend, whose child was diagnosed with ASD. It invites kids to communicate via image cards accompanied by text. The words on the cards are spoken out loud when they are tapped. You can create as many categories as you like (for instance, Food, People, Emotions) and choose images from the image bank or add your own. You can also record your voice and associate it with any cell you wish. For further information, see www.schmoontzapps.com

TECH FOR TRACKING GOALS AND OUTCOMES

The following apps can help you and your child stay on top of your goals (Rudy 2024b):

Birdhouse for Autism: Parents and teachers can use this app to set goals and monitor a child's progress in numerous areas, including behaviors, moods, and sleep. It works on desktop and laptop computers and comes in a free "lite" version as well as a more comprehensive one. This app can be downloaded on the Apple App Store or Google Play.

Autism Tracker Pro: This app uses visual icons to track goals related to therapeutic goals and outcomes, as well as mood and sleep. You can find this one on the Apple App Store.

TECH FOR SENSORY CHALLENGES

The following apps are centered on helping kids manage sensory challenges (Rudy 2023):

Miracle Modus: Designed for use with an iPad, this free app features imagery of hypnotic rainbows and soft bell sounds, which can be soothing for those wishing to mitigate sensory overload. Users can change or disable sounds, choose the modes they prefer, and email suggestions for display modes they would like to view. For further information, www.apps.apple.com/us/app/miracle-modus/

Calm: This meditation app, which is available on desktop, Google Play, and the Apple App Store, provides visual and verbal meditation and breathing sessions. It has a vast library of tools to help users relax and sleep better. The list of tools includes calming soundscapes and meditations. They help reduce anxiety, boost mood, increase confidence, and more. For further information, www.calm.com

Headspace: Similarly to Calm, this app has sessions that help kids (and adults) hone the basics of meditation to improve their focus, relieve anxiety and stress, and exercise mindful awareness. You can select areas you wish to work on, including anxiety, motivation, patience, generosity, and similar. For further information, see www.headspace.com

TouchPoints™: TouchPoints™ are patented wearables that use gentle vibrations to reduce the negative impacts of stress. There are many ways to wear the devices, so long as one is placed on the right and the other on the left of the body. For instance, they can be used on a belt, held in one's hands, or placed in pockets or socks. They can also be worn on the wrists or held in the hands. The wearables alter the body's stress response with BLAST (Bi-lateral Alternating Stimulation Tactile) technology. BLAST uses gentle, alternating vibrations on each side of the body to shift the brain from its default "fight or flight" response to its calm, in-control response. For further information, see www.thetouchpointsolution.com/pages/autism

TECH FOR MENTAL HEALTH

These apps focus on battling stress and improving mood (Medcalf 2017):

Super Stretch Yoga HD: Created for people aged four and up, this app features twelve yoga poses as well as "breathing breaks." It is available for iOS devices. Find it on the Apple App Store.

Relax Melodies: The Relax Melodies app is an intuitive tool that helps people sleep, focus, and relax. It contains a myriad of high-quality sounds and brainwave frequencies. It can be found on the Apple App Store or Google Play.

Chill Outz®: An app designed by child psychologist Jacqueline Vorpahl, it features numerous animated stories that teach kids techniques to stay mindful and relaxed in many situations. For instance, the story Buzzy Bee teaches kids how to relax by humming. Timid

Turtle teaches them how to overcome anxiety through muscular tension and relaxation, and Noisy Alien shows them how to remain calm in unfamiliar situations through body relaxation. For further information, see https://www.chilloutz.com/the-app

TECH FOR SOCIAL SKILLS AND EMOTIONAL REGULATION

This category of apps helps kids keep their emotions in check and focus on their goals (Common Sense Media 2024):

Breathe, Think, Do with Sesame: This free app from Sesame Street teaches kids about patience, self-control, problem-solving, and planning. An animated "monster" friend helps kids breathe slowly, come up with a plan for different situations (such as saying goodbye to their parents, sleeping in the dark, or waiting in line), and harness self-calming practices. For further information, see www.sesameworkshop.org/resources/breathe-think-do

Calm Counter Social Story & Anger Management Tool: Calm Counter is a visual and audio tool that helps kids calm down when they are feeling anxious or angry. It includes a social story about anger as well as various audio/visual tools for relaxation. You can find this app on the Apple App Store.

Daniel Tiger's Grr-ific Feelings: In order to manage their emotions, children have to first know how they are feeling and then learn how to express their emotions assertively and respectfully. This app helps kids identify and express their emotions through songs and games. For instance, kids can step into a photo booth and pose for photos displaying different emotions. They can also sing about them and draw them. For further information, see www.pbskids.org/apps/daniel-tigers-grr-ific-feelings.html

Social Stories Creator & Library: This app allows parents and teachers to create customized social stories to help kids learn and interact with others socially in a structured way. For further information, see www.touchautism.com/app/social-stories-creator-library/

Zones of Regulation: This app was created to help kids manage their emotions. It takes them through a town with different emotional zones (Blue, Green, Yellow, and Red). The Blue Zone features emotions like "sad," "tired," and "lonely." The Green Zone features emotions like "happy," "calm," and "ready to learn." The Yellow Zone features emotions like "upset," "worried," and "frustrated." The Red Zone features emotions like "mad," "scared," and "unsafe." For further information, see www.zonesofregulation.com

TECH FOR SAFETY

ICE4Autism App: This app was developed in collaboration with Autistic people for Autistic users. It provides first responders and medical personnel with information quickly and effectively for greater patient-centered medical care for people with Autism. It allows you to store information that is unique to the user, including how they communicate, their unique behaviors and triggers, special instructions, health conditions, and emergency contacts. For further information, see www.ice4autism.com

Life 360: Protect your child and other family members with this safety and location-sharing app, which is available for Android and Apple phones. Users can place alerts so they can see when someone has arrived home and tap the screen to send an SOS. For further information, see www.life360.com

Angelsense GPS Tracker: An assistive technology that includes a proactive monitoring and alerting system. It can be used to prevent wandering, stop bullying and mistreatment, and improve well-being. The tracker has a two-way voice system that allows you to speak to your child at any time and requires no action from your child. It also has a one-voice feature, so you can hear who your child is with. Visit the site to see testimonials from parents. Because the app allows parents to hear everything that is happening to their child and to track their exact location, it is a great ally to nip bullying and other types of abuse in the bud. For further information, see www.angelsense.com

Apple Air Tags: These small, coin-shaped devices help users locate personal belongings, and they can easily be attached to items like wallets, keys, bags, and other personal objects. Items can be found on Apple devices by using the Find My app. For further information, see www.apple.com/airtag/

HOW MUCH TECH IS TOO MUCH?

Studies show that Autistic children and youths spend more time using technology than neurotypical children across all time frames (days and evenings, weekdays, and weekends). They also show that both groups exceed current guidelines (Cardy et al. 2023). Around 50 percent of Autistic kids use technology for therapeutic purposes, though recreational use is also high. Autistic kids with high levels of screen media use tend to exclude other activities such as homework, socializing, and physical activity.

The good news is that despite concerns regarding screen time among Autistic children and youth, parents are generally more positive than negative about the impacts of technology on their children and their family's quality of life. They have also reported benefits from tech use in the improvement of social and motor skills, emotional regulation, and language and communication.

How, then, can you help your child strike a healthy balance so she doesn't overuse technology to the detriment of other key areas of her life? It starts by setting and respecting routines and scheduling a healthy amount of screen time. Use timers if needed to remind her when screen time is over. Aim to include numerous non-tech-based activities in her schedule, such as sports and special interest group meet-ups. Screen time should ideally take place only when she doesn't have the opportunity to socialize with others. Reduce the amount of time she is alone by organizing parent-child or whole-family activities such as playing sports outside or going for a walk along a scenic route. If you feel like she is currently spending too much time online, gradually reduce her dependence on technology by giving her the chance to take part in numerous activities she enjoys more. You can slowly add more non-screen-based activities to her schedule so she doesn't have to deal with the impact of drastic change.

End-of-Chapter Activity: Create a Digital Toolbox with Your Child

In this chapter, you have seen many tech tools, apps, and devices that may have piqued your interest. You may be at the stage where you'd like to think about purchasing a few and creating a customized digital toolbox alongside your child. If so, follow these steps and let her input lead the way:

1. Start by identifying your child's specific needs, challenges, and interests.
2. Look at the different tech categories offered in this chapter and think about which are most relevant to your child.
3. Set up the digital tools on your child's tablet or desktop. If you are considering using an AAC device, contact the developers and organize an evaluation for your child.
4. This is the step your child may enjoy much more. Set up personalized boards, make your schedule, and involve your child in taking photos that you can upload to your chosen apps. Write and record scripts for apps that allow you to do so, involving other members of the family if possible.

Apps can help your child hone key skills such as communication, socialization, and emotional control. They can also be considered powerful tools in your arsenal against bullying and other unacceptable behavior from other people. In the next chapter, we will focus on a highly important skill: building resilience against the challenges your daughter may face during her school years.

1: INNER STRENGTH

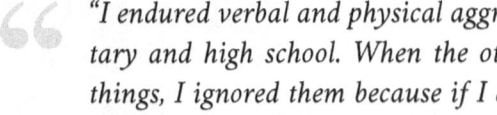

> "It may sound strange, but many champions are made champions by setbacks."
>
> — BOB RICHARDS (ERIEAU 2019)

In my first book, I shared that I had been sexually assaulted at school, and my story is shared by many Autistic women I have met since my diagnosis. Many have been bullied, some passive-aggressively and others more overtly. In this chapter, I will be addressing some of the hardest obstacles Autistic kids can face at school and discuss strategies they can use to boost their resilience. I'd like to start by sharing the stories of friends, students, and family members who have experienced bullying, assault, and other incidents at school.

> "I endured verbal and physical aggression throughout elementary and high school. When the other girls would say mean things, I ignored them because if I answered, it would become even worse. When they invaded my private space to see me 'go berserk,' I would push them away and run. One boy at school

was so persistent that I hit him hard with my knapsack, and he never bugged me again."

— BEATRICE, 23

"My classmates would make fun of how I dressed. When the girls in my group would say something, I would matter-of-factly answer them about the qualities of my clothing. I could tell it made them uncomfortable, but I would stay calm and not allow them to feel that they had made me feel bad about myself. I would flip it around and be like, 'What on earth are you talking about?'."

— MARIAH, 19

"When I was in the fifth grade, some kids who I thought were my friends tied my shoelaces together after asking me to close my eyes, and laughed their heads off when they saw me stumble. When I was in eighth grade, a girl I liked pretended to invite me to her house as a dare. Everyone at her table was laughing, and I realized she had no intentions of inviting me at all. It broke my heart because I really wanted to get to know her."

— EVAN, 35

"In sixth grade, a group of bullies cornered me at the back of the gym and pinned me to the wall. They lifted my skirt and started whipping me with rope. I burst into tears and felt so humiliated afterward, but I didn't tell anyone for days. I refused to go to school, and finally, I told my parents why. They reported the incident to the school, but that memory still traumatizes me."

— YASMIN, 51

> *"The worst incident I experienced was the hollering. When I would walk by a group of kids, they would yell insults at me. It got to the point that I would go the farthest possible route between my classroom and the lunch hall. One time the hollering got so bad I couldn't move and hugged a tree and cried in front of them. After that, one of them came and apologized, but I did not understand why they had been mean in the first place."*
>
> — PORTIA, 56

CHALLENGES FACED BY AUTISTIC GIRLS

Just a few challenges Autistic girls may face at school include:

- **Bullying:** Evidence shows over 60 percent of children and young adults with Autism experience bullying. School-aged kids with Autism and those from disadvantaged neighborhoods are more likely to be victims than other Autistic children (Autism Speaks, n.d.-e).

  The Anti-Bullying Alliance defines bullying as "the repetitive, intentional hurting of one person or group by another person or group, where the relationship involves an imbalance of power" (Anti-Bullying Alliance, n.d.). It can involve actions like teasing, ignoring, leaving someone out of games, spreading rumors, playing pranks on someone, pushing, hitting, or taking someone's things or money. These actions can harm Autistic kids in many ways, damaging their self-esteem and impacting their mental health, social skills, and progress at school (Raising Children, n.d.-b).

- **Mate Crime:** This form of crime occurs when someone befriends a vulnerable person to exploit them financially, physically, or sexually. Perpetrators take advantage of the fact that someone is lonely and gain their confidence for ulterior motives (Jones 2022).

- **Sexual Assault:** A recent study shows that nine Autistic women out of ten have been victims of sexual violence (Cazalis et al. 2022). Two-thirds of victims were children when they were assaulted, and around 75 percent of victims reported several aggressions. Young victims were at a higher risk of being revictimized and of developing post-traumatic stress disorder (PTSD). Autism also seems to be a "vulnerability factor" that can increase the chances of abuse. The study researchers, therefore, stressed the importance of educating potential victims to keep abuse at bay.
- **Discrimination:** In my first book, I discussed the fact that males are around three times more likely to receive an Autism diagnosis than females. Studies have shown that a lack of understanding and recognition of specific female Autistic traits could lead to inequalities that hinder the identification of Autistic girls and women (Brickhill et al. 2023). Gendered stereotypes about Autism can fuel misconceptions about ASD. They can also exacerbate masking and the sensation of "not fitting in" with society. Autistic girls' behaviors may not comply with those of their peers yet remain unaccounted for because of the absence of a diagnosis. Gendered views toward Autism and males may influence clinicians and lead to underdiagnoses or misdiagnoses, thereby increasing Autistic girls' risks of developing anxiety and depression. Bias and a lack of awareness may pose severe consequences for the well-being of Autistic girls, putting them at a disadvantage to males.

As you have seen, many hurdles can interfere with your child's well-being during their school years. I mentioned that being diagnosed was a big relief for me because it explained so much about how I felt and how I was treated at school. The choice of whether to obtain a diagnosis for your child is personal, but it is worth seriously considering.

Receiving a diagnosis lets you know the challenges your child may face, and you can begin taking steps toward mitigation early.

One of the most important ways to help your child is to give her the tools she needs to report bullying and sexual assault. That begins by observing her, listening to her, and asking her questions that can lead to disclosure. For instance, if you notice your daughter looks sullen, you can ask a direct question such as, "Did something happen today to make you feel sad?" You can also encourage her to open up by asking her about the best and worst moments of her day. Do this every day so you don't miss potentially important information.

Use social stories or picture books to highlight problems such as bullying at school. Sites like PA Autism (www.paautism.org) and Happy Learners (www.happylearners.info) have free social stories that show kids what bullying looks like and what they can do when it happens. Important strategies to teach your child include not showing the bully that she is scared, leaving the scene if she can, and reporting the bullying behavior to her teacher, parent, or another trusted individual. Go over these stories various times so she knows exactly what to do in the case of any type of harassment.

SETTING HEALTHY BOUNDARIES

Personal boundaries are limits that define what we are willing to accept and what we are not. They can be physical, emotional, sexual, material, time-related, spiritual, or workplace/school-oriented. For instance, one person may not be comfortable hugging someone they have just met, while another may love physical affection. One child may prefer not to lend others some of their things, while others may enjoy sharing. Having and expressing boundaries is important because they help us establish and maintain healthy relationships, prevent burnout and resentment, and protect our mental health (Papyrus, n.d.).

Because Autistic girls may have people-pleasing tendencies, they may lack an understanding of boundaries, leading to many social struggles. Let's get back to the DSM-5-TR's criteria for Autism, which include "Deficits in social-emotional reciprocity, deficits in nonverbal communication used in social interactions, and deficits in developing, maintaining, and understanding relationships across a variety of contexts" (Autism Speaks, n.d.-f). Licensed professional counselor Jessica L. Penot notes that when these deficits occur, it can be easy to violate others' boundaries and allow others to do the same (Penot 2023). She adds that because Autistic people can struggle to develop, maintain, and understand relationships, they may get so excited when someone seems to want to get close to them that they overlook boundaries and engage in toxic relationships. This is why it is so important to show your child how to set boundaries and respect those set by friends and family. Key strategies you can use to help your child feel confident about stating her boundaries include (Raising Children, n.d.-c):

- **Explaining in Simple Terms What Boundaries Are:** Tell your child that it is okay to say no and that when someone else says no, it is important to respect their wishes. You can create images, social stories, and role-playing scenarios to illustrate that it is okay to say things like:
    - "I don't do hugs, but I am happy to meet you."
    - "Sorry, this is my lunch money. I will not give it to you."
    - "I don't feel like playing that game right now, but maybe later."
    - "I can only play until four."
    - "I don't like that music very much."
    - "I get overwhelmed by loud sounds."
- **Modeling Boundary-Setting:** You can also help your child by setting clear boundaries. For instance, if someone in your home or social setting calls someone else a name, tell them that you are not okay with this behavior.

- **Teach Your Child About the Body and Unwanted Touch:**
Learning about the body and its different parts can help children understand and communicate about their bodies. You can use everyday moments (such as when your child is getting dressed) to name body parts and use books, songs, and other resources to do so. You can also discuss how the body changes as people mature.

    It is also important for children to know about the difference between girls' and boys' bodies and between children's and adults' bodies. Children also need to differentiate between public and private parts of the body and when it is okay to be naked vs. clothed. For instance, you can say, "In the bathroom, it's okay to be naked, and it's also okay to be naked when you are getting dressed, but when you come out of your room, it is important to wear clothes." Share information about appropriate places for privacy, such as the bathroom. For example, you can say, "When I use the toilet, I shut the door."

    The next step is to teach your child about personal boundaries. For instance, you can talk about "good touch" vs. "bad touch" to let her know what type of touching is okay and in what situation. For instance, a hug from a sibling or a good friend can be considered a "good touch," but a hug from a stranger is not. You can also teach her that it's not okay for others to touch her private parts unless the person is a parent/guardian helping her with tasks like bathing. Share the fact that adults do not need help with these tasks. Your child also needs to know that *she* decides what feels comfortable or uncomfortable. For instance, she may not want to be hugged, even by friends. Let her know that it is always okay to say "no."

Use all the tools you have, such as visuals, so your child fully understands these vital boundaries. If she is nonverbal, visual aids like pictures, charts, and symbols can provide a constant, clear reference for her. Make sure to model appropriate behavior and embrace consistent boundaries at home and in other settings. Children who are minimally verbal or nonverbal can benefit from stories, pictures, and other means of learning about boundaries. One study by researchers from Boston University found that minimally verbal Autistic children understand significantly more language than they can produce (Thompson 2023).

Finally, remember that boundaries are a two-way street. If your child is violating a boundary, ask her to stop doing so calmly and respectfully. For instance, if she takes an item that is not for playing with, you can tell her, "I'm going to ask that you put that back in its place." Give a brief explanation of why this boundary is in place. For example, you can say, "That knife is sharp, and it can cut you if it slips." If she complies, congratulate her, saying something like, "Way to go putting that back in the drawer. It's great that you keep yourself safe."

A blog post from the Autism Blog Treatment Center of America resonated deeply with me because it recommended that parents limit boundaries to matters having to do with safety and hygiene. In other words, before setting a boundary for their child, they should ask themselves, "Does this boundary I am about to set have to do with health and safety?" (Autism Blog Treatment Center of America 2023). Of course, many parents also see the value in setting boundaries regarding personal items. For instance, if a child takes a parent's watch or phone, it's perfectly okay to set material boundaries for their use.

GOAL-SETTING BUILDS RESILIENCE

From a young age, setting and achieving meaningful goals gives children insight into themselves and enables them to act consistently with their values. It boosts their confidence, making it easier to bounce back from disappointments and daily challenges (Zurich 2023). Help your child set goals without overwhelming her by choosing SMART goals. SMART is an acronym for Specific, Measurable, Achievable, Relevant, and Time-Bound. Below is an example of a SMART goal you can help your child set (North Shore Pediatric Therapy, n.d.):

- **Specific:** "I will say 'Help me' when handing an item I need to my parent."
- **Measurable:** "I will do so at least three out of five times I need help."
- **Achievable:** "This goal is achievable for me because I usually ask my parents for what I want."
- **Relevant:** "This goal is relevant to my needs because it helps me obtain the help I need."
- **Time-Bound:** "I will master this goal in two days."

Try to use this system for goals that mean something to your child. Ensure the goals are phrased clearly and concisely, and consider working on one goal at a time so your child does not feel overwhelmed. Give her decision-making powers regarding how her goals are achieved and which goals to set next.

SEEING SETBACKS AS PART OF GROWTH

In *Raising an Autistic Girl*, I stressed how helpful embracing a growth mindset can be when dealing with disappointments and setbacks. A growth mindset differs from a fixed mindset in that it espouses that all abilities and skills can be learned. It celebrates "failures" as well as successes because failure can be the greatest teacher one will ever have. Getting it wrong sometimes enables you to define areas to work on, craft a new strategy, and go after your goals step by step (Diff Not Less 2023). When you have a growth mindset, you care less if someone labels you negatively because you know that qualities like competence in any subject can be attained with effort and commitment.

Below is a table that illustrates the fixed vs. growth mindsets at work in different aspects of a child's life:

Aspect	Fixed Mindset	Growth Mindset
Learning New Skills	"I'm not good at this, so I should stop trying."	"I can improve with practice, even if it's hard at first."
Facing New Social Situations	"I'm not naturally good at socializing, so I'll never fit in."	"I can learn to enjoy social interactions over time if I keep trying."
Dealing with Mistakes	"Mistakes show that I'm not good enough."	"Mistakes are one of the best ways to learn because they show me what I need to work on."
Asking for Help	"If I ask for help, it means I am incapable."	"Everyone asks for help because we can all teach each other new things."
Reacting to Criticism	"Criticism means there's something wrong with me."	"Feedback helps me learn and adapt."
Making Friends	"I'll never have friends because I don't know how to connect with others."	"I can take small steps to build friendships and learn from each experience."
Coping with Change	"I can't handle change, so I should avoid it whenever possible."	"Change can be hard, but I can learn to adapt and manage my emotions over time."
Managing Social Anxiety	"I'll always feel anxious in social situations, and there's nothing I can do about it."	"I can practice strategies to manage my anxiety and build confidence."
Understanding Others	"I'll never understand how others feel because it doesn't come naturally to me."	"I can learn to better understand others' emotions and perspectives through observation and practice."

Possessing a growth mindset is a pillar of resilience because it enables you to celebrate mistakes and see that they do not define your identity. In my first book, I shared strategies that you can employ to help your daughter embrace the growth mindset. These included helping her set realistic goals, teaching her to focus on her strengths instead of her shortcomings, and encouraging her to join special interest groups. You can also show her how to embrace positive problem-solving skills. When she has a challenge, encourage her to brainstorm solutions, weigh the pros and cons of each potential solution, and choose the one she feels is the best option. Next, she can try it out and see how it worked for her, reflecting on how she can do things similarly or differently the next time.

Start slow and steady, taking as much time as your child needs to see setbacks in a more positive light. Anticipate that she may have meltdowns or setbacks, and if or when she does, remind her of how she can use the growth mindset to overcome difficult thoughts and emotions. For instance, you can calmly and reassuringly say, "I know you feel overwhelmed, but remember the last time. You took some deep breaths and thought about (your puppy) Ella. Let's try doing the same now." Once your child has calmed down, review the calming techniques that worked for her and practice them with her so they become like second nature to her when she's stressed.

Model a growth mindset in your own responses to challenges. When things don't work out for you, reflect on what you have learned from the experience and share it with your child. When others give you feedback, even when it's negative, talk about it at the dinner table and discuss the efforts you will make to do better. Your child may also enjoy hearing about other kids who have overcome fixed mindsets and embraced setbacks as a chance for growth. Discuss the growth mindset often, both in the context of your own life and that of your child. The more they practice positive thinking, the more likely it is to become a habit (Wingert 2024).

SHOWING YOUR CHILD THE VALUE OF SELF-COMPASSION

When you hear the words "self-compassion," your mind may conjure up ideas of feeling sorry for oneself. In fact, this quality simply involves being kind to yourself … as kind as you would be to a best friend or a loved one. Studies have shown that self-compassion can be an excellent buffer against the damage of perfectionism (Paulise

2023). Self-compassion is all about facing failure, insecurity, or mistakes in a completely different way. Instead of criticizing oneself, it works on building resilience and happiness. It is based on three main pillars: self-kindness, mindfulness of one's emotions and feelings, and understanding that mistakes are simply part of being human.

Self-compassion is a simple concept, yet it can be quite difficult to achieve if a child is used to comparing themselves to others and being self-critical. Help your child exercise self-compassion by encouraging her to observe how she responds to failure. Share the fact that setbacks can produce negative thoughts and emotions. However, let her know that she *can* accept these thoughts and emotions *without* over-identifying with them. For instance, she can learn to say, "I'm feeling sad now because I didn't do as well as I'd hoped in my test," without becoming consumed by this thought. She can take steps to be kind to herself and understand that everyone does worse than they had hoped at various points in life.

Simply remaining calm in the face of failure, rejection, and criticism can boost her well-being and make her more productive. This is in stark contrast to harsh self-criticism, which can impact children's self-confidence and turn failure into despair (Seppala 2014). It takes time to fully embrace self-compassion. Help your child do so by brainstorming different acts of self-kindness they can perform when they face stress, disappointment, and other tough emotions.

SELF-ACCEPTANCE AND RADICAL VISIBILITY

When conducting research into masking, Devon Price discovered that many other Autistic people use masking to appear "appropriate" in public, only to battle problems like self-harm or eating disorders in private (NPR 2022). In a podcast interview with Eric Gracía, Price noted that there is a strong link between Autism and eating disorders, with many Autistic people searching for "rules to follow" so they can be considered "good" or "appropriate." They can create very rigid rules around their work and behavior and crave rituals (including rituals around food) that give structure and discipline to their lives despite the harm these rituals cause.

In his book *Unmasking Autism*, Price walks readers through an exercise by Autistic life coach Heather Morgan (Price 2022). It's called the Values-Based Integration Exercise, and it is designed to help readers get in touch with the person they were *before* they started masking. The exercise involves thinking of five moments in one's life (throughout different ages and settings) in which one felt truly happy and fulfilled. It might be a time in which one was on a family vacation, working on a specific project, or partaking in a hobby. Those memories have a lot to say about what we truly value, be it self-expression, creativity, family, and more. It's a great way for all of us to reconnect with ourselves and celebrate our authenticity.

Price also recommends freeing oneself from the need to be constantly observing others and masking. You can help your child do so by encouraging her to tap into the things she loves doing and allowing her to stim if she wishes. You can tap into your creativity and design a dream bedroom for her. You can purchase "stim jewelry," comprising items like spinning rings and necklaces and chewable bracelets, for her. Price also stresses the value of embracing "radical visibility" or authentic self-expression through fashion. In a world that demands that children "be like everyone else," it can be immensely liberating to express one's authentic self through fashion.

Earlier, I also mentioned the idea of "strawberry people." These are the kids to whom your child can freely disclose their Autism-related needs without fear of judgment. All these suggestions are centered around one central idea—it is much easier for your child to love and accept themselves if they are encouraged to align their choices with their values, interests, wants, and needs. And you can play a big role in making it happen.

THE VALUE OF POSITIVE AFFIRMATIONS

Positive affirmations are positively loaded phrases that help people challenge unwanted thoughts. Far from being a time-wasting pursuit, they have scientifically proven benefits for mental health. Self-affirmation has three key ideas behind it. First, it helps us create a global narrative about ourselves, one in which we are flexible, moral, and capable of adapting to different circumstances. Second, it is based on the idea that maintaining our self-identity does not mean that we have to be exceptional, perfect, or excellent. All we need to do is be competent and adequate in the areas we personally value to be moral, flexible, and good. Finally, we maintain self-integrity by acting in ways that truly merit praise. So when we make a self-affirming statement like, "I am a hard worker," it's not because we simply want to receive that praise. It's because doing so makes us want to deserve that praise by acting in ways that are consistent with that personal value (Moore 2019). Just a few scientifically proven benefits of affirmations include:

- Reduced stress levels and rumination
- Greater motivation to increase physical activity
- An increased likelihood of making healthier food choices
- Positive academic achievement

If you're inspired to help your child create positive affirmations, see Activity Two below.

End-of-Chapter Activities:

Activity One: Circle of Friends

This activity helps your child understand personal boundaries. It involves drawing various "circles within a circle." The smallest (and most central) circle represents your child, and all the larger circles represent people in her life. The aim is to help her understand what her relationship is with different people, what behavior is okay, and how she should behave with them.

To complete this activity, your child will need a large piece of paper and various colored pens. Start with a small circle and ask her to draw a picture of herself in the middle of it. Next, draw a larger circle around this circle and ask her to write the names of those who are closest to her (for instance, her parents and siblings). She should then draw larger circles with the names of different groups of people, including extended family, best friends, acquaintances, professionals who help them, and strangers. Ask your child to color each circle and embellish it as she pleases (Raising Children, n.d.-d).

Once your child has completed their full circle of friends, ask them questions like:

- How would you say hello to people in each of these circles?
- Which of these people would it be okay to hug or kiss?/Which people can hug or kiss you?
- Who would you invite to your home for a visit or meal?
- Who would you talk to if you had a problem?
- Which of these people could pick you up from school?
- Which of these people could hold your hand?

Activity Two: Helping Your Child Replace Harmful Labels with Useful Ones

In her book *Raising Your Spirited Child*, author and parent educator Mary Sheedy Kurcinka encourages frustrated caregivers to reformulate the negative impressions they may have of their children (Kurcinka 2006). The author set out to challenge harmful labels such as "stubborn" by replacing them with new labels such as "assertive" and "persistent." Just a few other labels she replaces are "picky" with "selective," "demanding" with "knows what she wants," and "inflexible" with "traditional." You can help your child reformulate negative labels by asking her to think of hurtful words others may have used to describe her and replacing these words with more positive, beneficial labels. Use Kurcinka's template to inspire you (Price 2022):

Old Label	New Label
e.g., "loud"	e.g., "enthusiastic"

Activity Three: Creating Positive Affirmations

Encourage your child to create positive affirmations about herself. Work alongside her to use these affirmations to create posters, drawings, collages, and other creative works. Pin the works around your home so your child can be reminded of their value. I'm a bit of an affirmations fan myself, and I use a site called Mirrormerch (mirrormerch.co), which prints out gorgeous stickers to encourage self-love. I create my own customized labels, and the company prints them out. These stickers are all over the mirrors in our home, much to my wife's dismay!

Activity Four: Choosing Self-Care Behaviors

Using these five categories to start with, encourage your child to choose at least one behavior from each category to help her embrace the value of self-care. Introduce these activities into her weekly routine (The Autism Helper, n.d.):

- **Doing an Activity I Enjoy:** For instance, doing yoga, joining a special interest group, or drawing
- **Eating Healthy Food:** For example, eating fruits and vegetables

- **Practicing Good Hygiene:** For instance, taking a bath every evening, brushing teeth, styling hair
- **Practicing Self-Compassion:** For example, telling oneself it's okay to make mistakes
- **Learning Something New:** For instance, practicing new skills, learning a new subject, or trying to do a new chore

In this chapter, we've covered ways to boost your child's resilience. The next chapter is closely related to the topics we've covered, as it involves helping your child face anxiety and stress at school.

 NAVIGATING STRESS AND ANXIETY AT SCHOOL

> "Anxiety can be a major part of an Autistic girl's everyday life, especially when they are masking and trying their best to fit in. This may mean that they keep it together all day at school, so to teachers, there doesn't seem to be a 'problem.' This emotion and anxiety may all be released in meltdowns, shutdowns, or anxiety attacks when they get home."
>
> —AUTISTIC GIRLS NETWORK (AUTISTIC GIRLS NETWORK, N.D.)

ANXIETY IN AUTISTIC GIRLS

Anxiety is thought to affect at least 40 percent of Autistic individuals; it is also a prevalent issue for Autistic children and youths (McCaffrey 2018). A study led by Christine Wu Nordahl, director of the Autism Phenome Project, showed that Autism and anxiety may differ in girls. In particular, females exhibit higher rates of anxiety disorders than males, especially in patterns specific to Autism, such as fear of change. Girls also have higher rates of traditional forms of anxiety, such as social anxiety, generalized anxiety, and separation anxiety (Living on the Spectrum 2023). Children in this study with distinct anxieties showed slower growth in the amygdala (the brain's fear center) from the ages of three to eleven compared to children without anxiety. Those with traditional forms of anxiety, meanwhile, had a larger right amygdala than those with distinct anxieties or no anxiety.

Those of us with sensory processing disorder (SPD)—which affects the way the brain processes sensory information—lack the ability to adapt to new information. We don't do well with what "could happen." Instead, we prefer predictability. Yet our everyday lives constantly expose us to unpredictable input. As stated by writer Kelly Dillon, "The world is full of random, unusual, and unpredictable things. When you have a brain that struggles to make sense of the predictable—let alone the unpredictable—it's easy to understand why anxiety is the result" (Dillon, n.d.).

Research highlights the importance of diagnosing the type of anxiety a child has. Current therapist-led approaches include (National Autistic Society, n.d.-c):

- **Cognitive-Behavioral Therapy (CBT):** In chapter 6, I spoke about CBT as a way to help your child recognize, manage, and express thoughts and emotions. CBT shows individuals how to reframe negative thoughts into more positive ones based on experiences and available evidence. Just a few common beliefs that people with ASD can have include, "If I stay away from people, I won't get hurt," "If I try to make friends, I'll fail," and "I'm flawed/weird/out of control." These beliefs can stop them from achieving their goals because they can become self-fulfilling. By seeing themselves in a more realistic light, individuals can realize their potential and reach for meaningful goals (Grossman 2021).

    Another therapy that is sometimes employed is Acceptance and Commitment Therapy (ACT), which is considered a branch of CBT. As I wrote in chapter 3, ACT is centered on accepting things that cannot be changed and committing to changing things that can make one happier and healthier. This approach builds greater psychological flexibility, which can help kids deal with challenges and enhance their overall well-being (Wassner, n.d.).

- **Mindfulness Training:** This approach teaches children mindfulness techniques they can harness during sensory overload. It can involve various exercises that help children pay attention to what is happening in their minds and notice how it makes them feel (National Autistic Society, n.d.-c).
- **Exposure Therapy:** This type of therapy involves gradually exposing someone to the things that make them anxious so that, in time, the anxiety surrounding those things diminishes or disappears. In a clinical setting, the therapist teaches the client cognitive strategies before exposure to the things that can cause them anxiety. This empowers them to control their fears instead of allowing them to build up (Attwood & Garnett Events 2023).
- **Low Arousal Techniques:** This approach focuses on reducing stress. It identifies triggers and uses low-intensity strategies and solutions to avoid "punishing" distress. It is based on relationship building, trust, respect, and a philosophy of care. Without all these things, it is hard for a child to feel confident, secure, and safe. Techniques include reducing demands on a child, refraining from talking to them, giving them space, providing them with an escape plan, and employing exercise (National Autistic Society, n.d.-c).
- **Sensory Integration Training:** This approach relies on specific strategies created to help with sensory differences and tailored to a person's needs by an occupational therapist. The aim is to help your child handle multiple sensory inputs (Raising Children, n.d.-e).

In some cases, a medical professional may recommend medication such as anti-depressants. It is important to note that there is little research into whether these treatments help curb anxiety in Autistic people. Moreover, medication may produce side effects like irritability and drowsiness.

> *"I have had horrible anxiety since I was a kid. I cannot bear noise or bright lights, and music is very annoying, yet it is hard to escape. I sometimes have panic attacks if I go to a mall or anywhere with music and people talking loudly. I just want to escape."*
>
> — BELÉN, 19

> *"I'm in my thirties now, but elementary and middle school were tough. I had severe anxiety and panic attacks almost every day. From the age of nine, I was homeschooled, which was a huge relief. Over time, I've noticed my generalized anxiety has decreased, which I think is partly because I have more control over my surroundings and what I'm exposed to. These days, I have specific anxieties and phobias, like a fear of heights and social anxiety. I limit my days out to walking my dogs and meeting a couple of close friends who are also on the spectrum. I have sensory processing disorder, and sometimes, I feel like I cannot handle all that is going on around me. When that happens, I just shut down and need to be on my own. I do yoga and that helps ground me when I'm feeling stressed out. I know that I am super lucky to be able to work from home and only be around people I am comfortable with."*
>
> — LILA, 34

HOW CAN YOU HELP YOUR CHILD?

In addition to seeking professional help, you can also adopt strategies at home to help your child battle anxiety.

Identifying Triggers

Start by helping your child identify her triggers. Encourage her to keep a journal and keep one of your own, noting down the events that were taking place before she experienced anxiety and panic or before she shut down or had a meltdown.

Self-Soothing

Encourage your child to self-soothe in the way that works best for her, be it through fidget toys, rocking, or listening to music. The sensory tool kit recommended in chapter 5 can also be of great help when your child is feeling stressed or anxious.

Visual Schedules

Because changes in routine can be so stressful for Autistic girls, use visual schedules to reduce uncertainty. Remember to incorporate new activities into her schedules as early as possible so she is ready for them when they arise.

Good Sleep

Remember to prioritize good sleep for your child. It is much harder to manage stress and anxiety when one feels tired or sleepy during the day. Studies indicate that lack of sleep is, in itself, a risk factor for anxiety, and it increases the likelihood of depression (Harvard Sleep Medicine, n.d.).

Relaxation Methods

Earlier, I recommended techniques like meditation and breathing to help your child self-soothe. Remind her to use them and practice them as part of her routine so that techniques like controlled breathing are second nature to her. In chapter 5, I mentioned apps like Calm Kids, which can help soothe a child experiencing sensory overload. Other apps you may want to try include Miracle Modus (which uses visual patterns and sounds to reduce anxiety and stress) and Colorfy (a calming coloring app) (Rudy 2024b).

Visual Communication Supports

Visual communication supports such as the Picture Exchange Communication System® (PECS®) empower kids who may not communicate verbally to ask for what they want using pictures. You can use these cards to help your child respond when she is feeling stressed or anxious. Social stories, images, and artistic projects can also help her express, process, and deal with stress.

BATTLING SOCIAL ANXIETY

Autistic people have significantly higher rates of social anxiety, with one study showing that social anxiety disorder is the most common anxiety disorder among Autistic people (Sarris 2018). Our difficulties with understanding social cues, participating in conversations, maintaining eye contact, recognizing emotions, and interpreting nonverbal cues, like body language and expressions, can lead us to dread social occasions like parties and (in the case of children) playdates. Other factors, such as a preference for predictable situations, a tendency toward rigid thinking patterns, and sensory challenges, can also make it harder to be present and relaxed in social settings.

In addition to this blend of factors, we should also take the double empathy problem into account. In the introduction to this book, I mentioned that this concept stipulates that Autistic people have difficulty understanding the communication and perspectives of neurotypical people, and neurotypical people have difficulty understanding the communication and perspectives of Autistic people (Reframing Autism, n.d.). That is, although it is often erroneously stated that we do not have empathy, empathy is actually a two-way street. Because of our differences, it can be hard for neurotypical people to empathize with our way of communicating, expressing our emotions, interacting with others, and sensing the world around us. While it is often said that we lack "social insight," others can also lack insight into our culture and our way of thinking and being.

Neurotypical people can assume that their familiar way of empathizing is superior to ours. They can conclude that *we* need to learn and communicate with *them*. However, they may not hold themselves to the same standards by trying to learn *our* perspectives. As a result, many Autistic people gain a greater level of insight into neurotypical behavior than vice versa.

Sometimes, only our family or friends try to understand the way we think, feel, and behave—and our wants and needs. This is one of the reasons why connecting with other Autistic people and sharing our experiences can feel so reaffirming. Writer Sarah Meyer, who is Autistic, states, "There is a kind of collective reframing that happens when Autistic people get together and tell stories; we come to realize that there is often a strong logic and meaning to the way we do things" (Meyer 2024b).

A child who has been rejected and bullied many times over can go quiet and avoid engaging with others. When they have to be at school, speak in class, or attend social occasions with their families, they may develop an immense fear of saying or doing the "wrong" thing (Montaser et al. 2023). There is another important point to note: Autistic people can often feel more socially anxious around family and close friends than people they don't know as well. This may seem counterintuitive, but it makes a lot of sense. Finding unconditional friends can take many years. When we find them, we want to make sure that we don't lose them. What's more, our interactions are often structured and repetitive, and we hope that they are okay with this and that it is still acceptable to be ourselves with them.

"Whenever I meet my friend Karina, we always do the same thing. We meet at the beach and sit on the shore, and I like to watch and listen to the waves. Sometimes, I like to be quiet and watch them. Karina knows this and does not talk to me too much. Sometimes I wonder if she is bored, but every week, she meets me, and I am always excited about seeing her."

— MILA, 17

If you feel your child might have social anxiety disorder, consider seeking help from her pediatrician, who can refer you to a mental health practitioner. The latter may recommend CBT or other therapies that can help her feel more comfortable in social settings. Getting help can ensure she makes the most of her school experiences, since children with social anxiety can refrain from joining classroom discussions and forming part of friendship groups.

You can support your child in many ways, starting with recognizing her triggers and showing her that you accept and understand when she is feeling anxious. Share instances of when you may have felt anxious in your childhood so she knows she is not alone. Encourage her to replace harmful beliefs with positive ones. For instance, if she says something like, "Nobody will want to play with me," you can ask, "How do you know they won't want to play with you? Remember the last party we went to, and how Jenny was talking to you about comics? Maybe you will meet someone nice again tomorrow."

Many of the strategies I suggested earlier in this book, such as using social stories, can help her feel more comfortable about attending play dates and other social events. You can also role-play a few simple scenarios in which she can practice saying hello, saying her name and school year, or talking about her hobbies. If your child finds it hard to talk to people, encourage her to say just one thing—perhaps "goodbye" after an event is over. If you are present, try not to label your daughter as "shy" in front of others. If anyone calls her shy, you can boost her confidence by saying something like, "Actually, she is a chatterbox once she gets to know people." If your child is feeling anxious in a social situation, don't force her to remain in it. It may be more beneficial to go home, recoup, and practice gently and calmly for her next social event (Raising Children, n.d.-f).

You can also do wonders by ensuring your child has access to people she can freely disclose her Autism to if she wishes, without any fear. Embrace structure and simplicity. For many of us, it's more enriching to hang out with a small but loyal group of friends than try to fit in with a large group of acquaintances we have to "perform" for.

End-of-Chapter Activities:

Activity One: Progressive Muscle Relaxation

If your child is feeling anxious, this exercise may help her relieve tension (Children's Hospital of Philadelphia, n.d.).

Ask your child to lie down in a comfortable spot, such as the sofa or a bed. Tell her that she will be tightening and relaxing different parts of her body. Start with her feet, asking her to point her toes toward the ceiling and squeeze the muscles in her feet as tight as she can for about five seconds. Then ask her to let all the tension go and to feel her feet becoming relaxed and heavy. Move up the body, focusing on different muscle groups such as the legs, stomach, arms and hands, shoulders, and face. For each of these main groups, use metaphors to help her focus on squeezing and relaxing her muscles. The following metaphors may serve as inspiration:

- **Legs:** "Squeeze your legs tight, like you're pretending they are hard tree stumps. Hold it for five seconds … and relax."

- **Stomach:** "Pull your tummy in, like it's a treasure chest and you're locking it very tight. Hold it ... and relax."
- **Arms and Hands:** "Pretend you're squeezing a ball in your hands. Squeeze it tightly. Hold it ... and relax."
- **Shoulders:** "Raise your shoulders toward your ears, like you're a turtle hiding in its shell. Hold it ... and relax."
- **Face:** "Squish your face like you've just bitten into a super sour lemon. Hold it tight ... and relax."

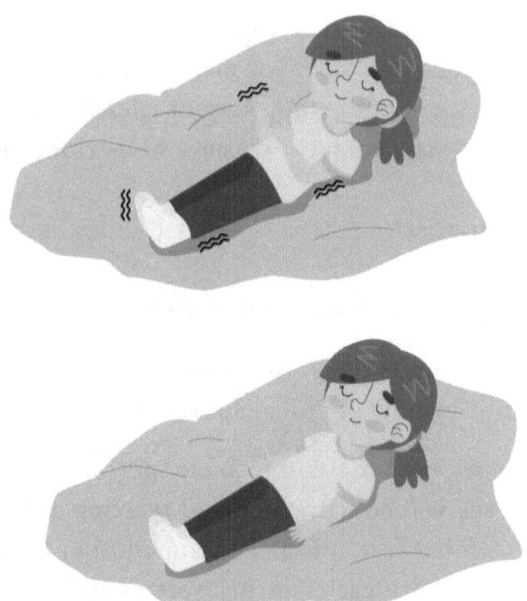

After this, guide your child to take a few deep breaths. Now ask them if they feel a little more relaxed than before they did the exercise.

Activity Two: Cognitive Reframing Exercise

This exercise aims to help your child replace negative, harmful beliefs with more positive ones. Take your child's journal and encourage her to write down negative thoughts. Next, ask her to think of a happier response to these thoughts. I have provided you with a few examples below (Autism Teaching Strategies 2014):

Unhelpful Thoughts	Happy Thoughts
"I will always be lonely."	"Many people love me."
"There is something wrong with me."	"I am the sum of many good things."
"I'm a loser."	"I have many things I like about myself, like how well I can draw."
"That kid bumped into me on purpose."	"Maybe it was an accident."
"They won't play with me because I'm dumb."	"I'm not dumb. There are things about me that other kids might like."

Activity Three: Mindfulness Strategies

Introduce your child to mindfulness activities such as (Swain 2022):

- **Sound Meditation:** Introduce your child to a chime or singing bowl. Invite her to play the bowl and describe what she hears. Ask her to close her eyes while you play the bowl. Invite her to listen for the vibration of the chime. When the chime stops, ask her to pay attention to any other sounds in her environment for between one and three minutes. Start with sounds that are far away and end with sounds that are in or near the room. Ask her to listen to her own body. Can she hear herself breathing or her heart beating? Ask her to share what she has heard.
- **Mindful Eating:** Invite your child to play a game in which she pretends that she has found an item of food (say M&Ms) on an alien spaceship. Invite her to inspect the candy, smell it, and feel how it rolls upon the palm of her hand. Invite her to feel how it tastes and feels in her mouth, then to bite into it. Tell her to notice the sounds or sensations that chewing makes and to pay attention to what it feels like when she swallows the candy.

- **Mindfulness Script for Anxiety:** Read the following script while playing soothing nature music if your child enjoys it. Ask her to sit or lie down in a comfortable spot while you read her the script. If she likes the script, consider recording it so she can play it whenever she wants to:

    Take a deep breath in, like you're smelling a flower. Breathe out, like you're blowing out a candle. Let's do that two more times—big breath in, long breath out.

    Imagine you have a little ball of worry in your tummy. It is there because it wants to protect you, but sometimes it talks too much. Now take the ball in your hands and say, "Thank you, but I've got this!" Lift the ball into the sky and watch it slowly fly away. Picture it getting smaller and farther as you breathe. Now, put your hand on your tummy. Feel it go up as you breathe in, and down as you breathe out.

    Up ... and down. Breathe in slowly. Now breathe out. (Repeat this to your child slowly five times.)

    If your mind starts to wander to other thoughts, that's okay. Just come back to your breath, gently, like a butterfly landing on your hand. When you're ready, open your eyes and give yourself a little hug. You just got rid of the worry ball. That's amazing!

Anxiety is a difficult hurdle faced by many Autistic and neurotypical children. If your child is battling anxiety, consider enlisting the help of professionals in therapies like CBT. In the next chapter, we will turn our eye to the future, ensuring your child has a smooth transition into adolescence and beyond.

E: ENVISIONING THE FUTURE

> *"The days go slowly, but the years go fast."*
>
> — ANONYMOUS (POWERS 2013).

When your child is an infant or a toddler, the days can drag on. You may wonder when you'll ever have a good night's sleep, enjoy a full day all to yourself, or even find just an hour to go to the gym. Yet all too soon, your child is in high school, and you realize that in no time at all, they will be out in the world forging their path, armed with all the lessons, advice, and love you gave them.

When your daughter struggles at school or with friendships, it can seem like a constant uphill battle—not just for her but also for you! You want her to enjoy unique childhood experiences, like the sense of camaraderie or the confidence from excelling in a specific subject at school. By the same token, these years can be immensely fulfilling because, during this time, you can see how all the efforts your child has made *are making a difference*. And you have a big role to play in her progress.

When I am socializing with moms of Autistic kids, we often share our stories and find inspiration from each other's experiences and achievements. We know how our children's different ways of seeing the world can be a big advantage in many areas of life, and there are countless stories that back this fact. But raising a child is about more than just helping them achieve their professional and personal dreams. It's also about teaching them how to be happy.

In earlier chapters, I've shared information about helping your child enjoy and thrive in elementary school. In this chapter, we will look toward the future, with strategies to help your child face major changes in her life.

PREPARING YOUR CHILD FOR HER TRANSITION TO MIDDLE SCHOOL

As you help your daughter make her way through numerous schedules, tests, and social challenges, you may wonder how she will survive the increasingly complex schedules, schoolwork, and social pressures that middle school can bring. Middle school can be a bit of a battleground for children, yet there are many strategies you can embrace to make things better. While every child has their specific wants and needs, the following strategies may make your child feel more empowered (Palmer, n.d.):

- **Prepare as early as possible.** Parent and writer Ann Palmer gives excellent advice regarding how to navigate a full-inclusion middle school education. She suggests that when a child is in the fourth or fifth grade, parents should consult a guidance counselor from a middle school or parents of middle school kids. The aim is to ask what skills kids need in middle school and use the information obtained to create an IEP that takes this information into account. She also recommends that the IEP meeting regarding a child's transition to middle school should take place in a middle school rather than an elementary school. Moreover, a regular education teacher should be present.

- **Create a color-coded schedule containing all your child's classes and laminate it, placing the schedule on the cover of your child's daily diary or notebook.** Try to obtain the schedule of classes as early as possible, using social stories or visuals to illustrate the transition between classes.

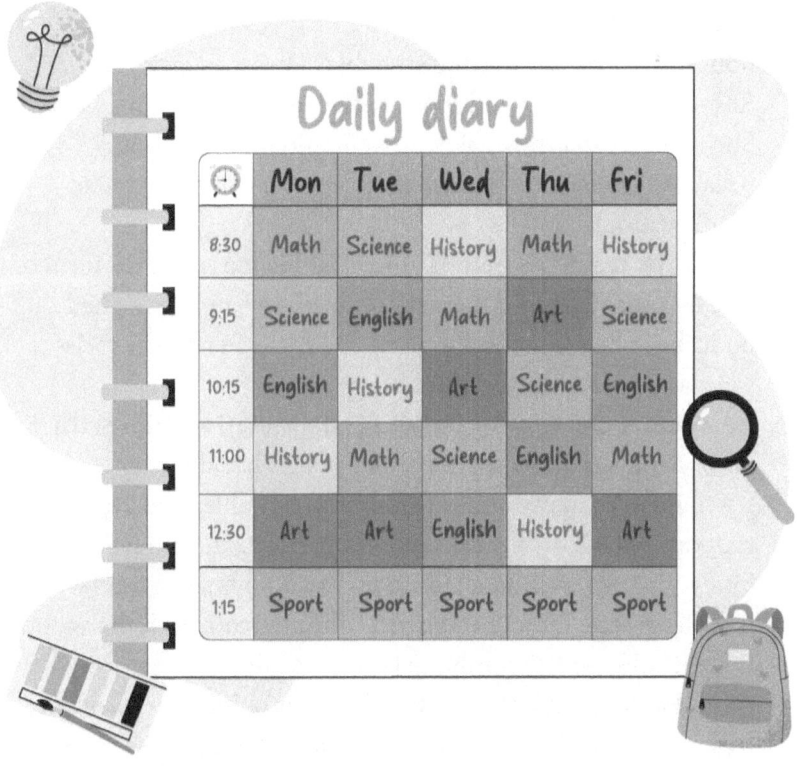

- **Access tools that can make day-to-day life at school easier for your child.** For instance, writer Palmer used one notebook with dividers (instead of various notebooks) to help her son organize his schoolwork. She also accessed a lock that he found easier to use than a traditional spin dial lock. She additionally asked for an extra set of textbooks for home, since it can be a challenge for kids to get all pertinent books and notebooks home every day. She mentions that in her son's middle school, highlighted textbooks were available. These textbooks, which were highlighted by the school's PTA, helped her son understand what to focus on. The use of highlighted books can also be placed in your child's IEP.

- **Get to know your child's school as well as possible, to identify any extra resources or facilities that could be useful.** Palmer states that in her son's school, most kids with learning difficulties were located in a specific hall that also housed academically gifted students. There, an extra LD Resource teacher would move between classes and help kids. She explains that this hall was well-suited to her child, because the teachers there were prepared to make needed modifications.
- **Enlist the teacher's help if your child is particularly fond of one or more kids.** Perhaps these children can be assigned as buddies or be placed in the same classes as her so she feels safer and more comfortable.
- **Remember the tips for building good relationships with your child's teachers.** The school year is usually very busy, so try to meet as many of her teachers as possible. Create rapport, decide on a means of communication, and let staff know what your child needs to learn and manage stress well in a classroom. Don't hesitate to communicate with the school if you find specific stumbling blocks causing distress for your child. Palmer, for instance, asked for her child to be exempted from physical education classes because these classes were distressful for him. Remember that your child and her well-being come first.

PREPARING FOR PUBERTY

Puberty begins at the age of around ten to eleven for girls, and it involves changes and transitions that parents can help their daughters prepare for. When speaking with your daughter about this phase, start by explaining that puberty is the transition from a child's body to a grown-up one. Don't hesitate to make clear statements like, "When you enter puberty, you grow hair in your underarms," or "When you enter puberty, your breasts grow." Use unequivocal language and avoid metaphors that may confuse your child. For instance, instead of saying, "You may start breaking out," you can say, "You may develop pimples." Encourage her to ask questions about puberty, even if they are awkward. Remember that you don't need to know all the answers. If she asks you about something you don't know, just say, "Oh, I don't know that; let's look it up!"

Books, images, and social stories can all help her understand what is happening to her and the difference between how girls and boys develop. You may find it useful to craft a social story containing statements like:

- My body will grow and change.
- My body might look different. I might grow taller. My hips might get wider. That is perfect.
- I will get new hair on parts of my body, like under my arms and between my legs. That happens to everyone when they grow up.
- My body will do new things. I might get my period. That means my body is healthy. I can learn how to take care of myself during this time.
- My skin might change. I might get pimples or oily skin. That is normal.
- My emotions might feel big and hard to control sometimes. That is part of growing up, too.

- Everyone's body grows differently and at its own speed, and that is okay.

Now is also a good time to bring out periods. Most girls get their first period between the ages of eleven and fourteen-and-a-half, though periods can arrive anywhere between nine and sixteen years of age (Raising Children, n.d.-g). You may notice that your daughter has a growth spurt or begins to grow hair in her underarms. These are signs that her period may be just around the corner. In the same way that you discuss changes that occur during puberty, you can bring up periods. The following social story may inspire you to share information about what happens at this stage of life:

- As my body changes, I will get my period.
- That means that a small amount of blood will come out of my vagina. This is normal and happens to all girls when they grow up.
- I will need to use special underpants, a pad, or a tampon to protect my clothes.
- Periods usually come every twenty-eight days, but sometimes they come a bit earlier or later, and that is okay.
- A few days before I get my period, I might feel more irritable, angry, or sad.
- When I have my period, my ovaries, tummy, lower back, breasts, and sometimes even my legs can hurt, but I can take medicine for that. I can also use a hot water bottle for the pain.
- My period will last about four to seven days. If it lasts longer than seven days, I should talk to a trusted adult about it.

It can also help to give your child a kit they can take in their knapsack. This kit can contain sanitary pads, period-proof underpants, or tampons. If the kit contains sanitary pads or tampons, include a clean pair of underwear. You can also show them where these items are at home so they are accessible when your child needs them. Before your child's period starts, consider creating a visual schedule at home to change their pads, underwear, or tampons. Finally, show your child how to use a calendar app so they can more or less calculate when their next period is due.

BOOSTING YOUR CHILD'S INDEPENDENCE

Challenges in the areas of social functioning and communication, alongside repetitive behaviors and difficulties in attention and imitation, can limit an Autistic person's ability to watch others to learn the skills they need to be independent. Moreover, challenges with executive functioning can make it harder to solve problems that require one to plan and identify steps that need to be followed. Children may be used to having an adult by their side helping them with tasks, but when an adult is not present, they may find these activities difficult to complete. In a study published in the *Journal of Autism and Developmental Disorders*, researchers note that the ability to regulate or manage one's behavior can be considered one dimension of executive functioning. This particular domain includes initiation (starting an activity), monitoring one's behavior, and evaluating one's behavior (Hume et al. 2009).

They note that initiating an activity (like starting a homework assignment) can be difficult for Autistic kids because of difficulties with planning, processing speed, attention to relevant stimuli, motivation, and unclear expectations. Moreover, when Autistic people do not initiate or seek out social and verbal learning opportunities, they can miss out on opportunities to gain valuable information from others and their environment. They may also refrain from asking for help when they need it.

Kids may master a skill with one person in one location but find it difficult to generalize and apply this skill to other situations. They sometimes have difficulties relating new stimuli to past experiences because of their highly specific memory and the challenges they face with integrating new experiences. The authors conclude that formal interventions that can help a child increase their independence are those that shift from continuous adult management (for instance, paraprofessional support) to alternative stimuli that can provide cues and information they need to perform tasks.

Specifically, they found that self-monitoring, video modeling, and individual work systems can help children adapt their behavior, socialize, and improve their organizational skills. Self-monitoring involves focusing on one's own behavior to increase desired behaviors. Video modeling involves watching videos featuring a model who performs a target skill while being videotaped. These videos are short, lasting two to four minutes. They can be watched by the Autistic person when they need to perform specific tasks. Finally, independent work systems involve the use of "task baskets" that are set up with a schedule. They tell the child what they have to do first and next, and there is a visual at the end indicating what to do when they have finished. For pencil and paper tasks, children can use a notebook system instead of bins.

These systems allow children to work alone without adult interference, giving them a sense of accomplishment. What's more, they can be adapted to introduce new tasks in a variety of settings. They were developed by Division TEACCH®, which offers clinical services for Autistic people of all ages, plus numerous training (virtual and in person) and consultation programs to professionals who work with individuals on the Autism spectrum (TEACCH® Autism Program, n.d.). TEACCH® work systems are implemented in some schools (both regular and special), as well as intervention centers and schools with Autism-specific programs. I advise you to research schools in your area and to talk to the team of professionals aiding your child (including occupational therapists) for recommendations on interventions that can boost your child's independence.

You can also do your share at home by teaching them specific skills (covering areas like self-care, household chores, cooking, room organization, transport, community safety, money, and even vocational skills). Coping skills, which involve recognizing when something is bothering them and managing their thoughts and emotions, are also vital.

Tools like picture cards and social stories will once again come in handy, as will giving your child plenty of opportunity to practice the skills they have learned independently. When teaching your child new skills, break them down into smaller, manageable steps and create visual schedules in the spaces your child uses to perform these tasks. For instance, to do the laundry, your child might benefit from seeing visuals containing the following steps (McHugh 2024):

1. Separating colored clothing from whites
2. Loading the washer
3. Adding detergent
4. Starting the machine
5. Sorting the clothes and placing dryer-safe clothing into the dryer

I have emphasized the importance of routines throughout this book, and they are just as important when it comes to independence. The more a child performs vital routines such as bathing, getting dressed, making their bed, or preparing a meal, the more confident they can feel in their ability to carry out these tasks alone.

When children turn twelve, they can have a Community-Based Skills Assessment—a tool that was developed for the group Autism Speaks to help parents and professionals assess the current skill levels and abilities of people with Autism, starting at age twelve and continuing into adulthood. The assessment covers skills in areas like home life, transportation, personal finance, peer relationships, health and safety, and more key categories (Autism Speaks, n.d.-g).

In addition to teaching your child practical skills, when your child turns fourteen, it is a good age to include vocational skills in her IEP. Use her strengths and interests to guide the type of vocational activities that can be included as objectives. Help her start thinking about her goals for the future. Her CSA assessment will help you evaluate her skills and abilities to design an individualized plan that will serve her when she is an adult (Mulligan, n.d.).

ENCOURAGING SELF-ADVOCACY

Self-advocacy begins by developing an awareness of our thoughts and emotions. This is because when a child can say things like "I'm scared" or "I'm overwhelmed," they let others know their wants and needs, which is what self-advocacy is all about. To help your child tell you how she feels, you can start by observing her and commenting, "You are happy" or "You are scared," so she learns the words that describe how she is feeling in a given moment. You can also show her drawings and pictures of faces and ask for her help in identifying the emotion they are expressing.

Another strategy is to use cards that pair emotions with regulating activities. For instance, you could have a card with a smiling face on the left and the text "I am happy" beneath it. On the right side of the card, you could give the child two optional activities for when they feel that emotion, with the text "I can ask for …" written above it. The activities (which should also be represented with images or pictures) can include "a high five" or "a hug" (Reed 2022). Your child's occupational therapist can also help her identify coping strategies she can use when she is stressed or undergoing sensory overload.

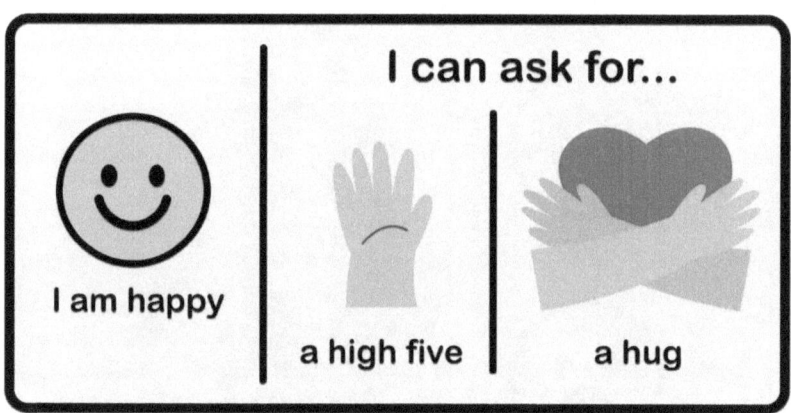

You can empower your child by giving her choices in various areas of her daily life, from the food your family eats to your outings or the games you enjoy together. Show her that her opinion matters by including her in decision-making settings, including IEP and similar meetings. Doing so will show her that her voice matters when it comes to making decisions that affect her life.

Be the best role model possible by showing your child that you look after yourself and express your wants and needs assertively, both in everyday situations and when you are resolving conflicts. It may take time until your child feels confident enough to stand up for herself, but by empowering her with self-advocacy skills, you can help boost her future confidence, independence, and personal growth (Cailuns 2024).

Throughout your daughter's childhood, build a team around her that can help her communicate, work independently, and grow in confidence. Bear in mind that there is no "right" way to do most things. It's more about finding a way to complete tasks and achieve goals that are meaningful and comfortable for her. I have mentioned the work of SLPs, OTs, and therapists. You may also find it useful to tap into the work of other professionals, including dietitians, who can provide invaluable help when it comes to helping children consume a healthy, nutritious diet despite having food sensitivities.

Developmental educators, who work in some schools to tailor programs to Autistic children, can help with social and coping skills at school, developing routines as a means to manage sensory challenges, address learning and communication difficulties, and more. Disability support workers can also help them develop independence skills and improve their daily living. For instance, they can support kids with daily activities, suggest useful community activities, and help them develop independent life skills. Disability support workers usually provide their services in person, either in the home or in a community environment, overseeing one-on-one or small group sessions (The Spectrum, n.d.).

PREPARING FOR YOUR CHILD'S ACADEMIC FUTURE

It's never too early to research different educational options, including colleges. Doing so will be useful if you are thinking of setting up a college fund, as you can have an idea of what tuition will cost. Research the useful services offered by different universities. My research has revealed that the list of US universities with specific accommodations for Autistic students includes:

- UCLA
- Rochester Institute of Technology
- Drexel University
- Syracuse University
- University of Texas at Austin
- Rutgers University
- University of Connecticut
- Carnegie Mellon University
- University of Washington.

The above list is not exhaustive or definitive since services may continue to change as the years go by. As a general rule, the types of services some of these universities offer include academic accommodations, volunteer opportunities, and opportunities for social connection (Apex ABA Therapy 2024d). Once your child chooses a college, the next step is for her to communicate with its disability services office so they can help her obtain the accommodations and support systems she needs. These services will help her with everything from finding suitable accommodation to different resources available on campus.

GETTING YOUR CHILD EXCITED ABOUT FUTURE CAREER OPTIONS

It's never too early to get your child excited about possible professions that suit her strengths and interests. Doing so can involve something as simple as sharing books and videos featuring different professionals. If your child has a special interest, perhaps she would enjoy volunteering for an organization that allows her to dive into it. You can also talk about your own career as well as those of close friends and family. Pictures and short videos can help your daughter see what a typical day is like for different professionals.

Every child will develop interests and skills as they grow, so generalizing is of little use. However, just a few of the many strengths many Autistic people display include excellent attention to detail, an ability to focus deeply on an area of interest, and strong visual thinking skills. We can be highly analytical, which can attract us to work in STEM professions (like IT, science, or archival work) or creative professions (such as art, photography, and design). Autistic girls can also be strongly attracted to animal care. This type of job often allows them to embrace a predictable routine and undertake structured tasks, which can be satisfying (Apex ABA Therapy 2024c).

Those who enjoy taking things apart and putting them together, meanwhile, may greatly enjoy working in computer troubleshooting, appliance and building repair, or vehicle mechanics. Temple Grandin provides a useful list of job types suited to visual, non-visual, and nonverbal thinkers. It is available online on the website of the Indiana Resource Center for Autism. Grandin also includes a list of "bad jobs" she considers difficult to undertake (Grandin 1999).

When discussing professions with your child, let her know about the many valuable qualities she can bring to a work environment, including her attention to detail, creativity, and logical thinking. Discuss important topics like diversity, and let her know that she can play a vital role in creating more diverse and inclusive environments. Get her excited about the many achievements of other Autistic people. Share the amazing achievements of writers, teachers, and animal welfare professionals like Temple Grandin. As much as possible, try matching the people you discuss with her specific interests. For instance, if she loves gaming, tell her all about Satoshi Tajiri, the creator of Pokémon. His intense focus and passion for gaming gave life to one of the most well-loved characters in the industry. Now, here's a fascinating anecdote your child may love to know: Tajiri was a passionate insect collector as a child, which led his classmates to call him "Dr. Bug." His love of collecting insects directly inspired the concept of catching and collecting Pokémon, an interest that has come to resonate with millions (Cardaro 2023).

ESTATE PLANNING FOR YOUR CHILD

I know you have so much to organize and many people to meet to help your child navigate their school life successfully. However, it is also important to plan your estate to ensure your child has the support they may need in the long term. To ensure your affairs are watertight, consider hiring an estate planning attorney who can advise you on matters such as setting up a special needs trust. Legal arrangements can be crafted to protect your child's eligibility for government benefits (such as Medicaid or SSI) and provide her with income that can help cover her care and support needs.

Choose a well-reputed, recommended professional who can help you make important decisions, such as guardianship and other long-term care arrangements. All parents can benefit from making a will and planning their and their children's financial future. Maximize any government benefits your child may be entitled to, including government programs like Medicaid, Supplemental Security Income (SSI), and Social Security Disability Insurance (SSDI). Review your estate plan regularly to ensure that it continues to match your child's needs (Santa Barbara Estate Planning & Elder Law, n.d.).

End-of-Chapter Activity: Career Vision Board

Create a vision board or collage that centers on careers your child is interested in. Work alongside her, inviting her to go through magazines or online sites. Print out images of professions, working environments, tools, and other inspirational imagery. Grab a large piece of cardboard your child can glue her images to. Encourage her to show her board to friends and loved ones and to share a bit about the images she chose.

In this chapter, we've been through the many considerations to make when planning for your child's future. Next, we'll wrap up the main ideas I shared throughout this book so you can have a quick refresher on everything you have read.

CONCLUSION

Your daughter's elementary and secondary schooling will take up twelve years of her life, and that means you have time to discover, work at, and perfect the many strategies I have shared with you throughout this book. I hope that throughout her (and your) journey, you keep the growth mindset at the forefront of your efforts. When I look back on my own trajectory and those of family and friends, I see that not everyone's road has been smooth and predetermined from the start. Many began their academic careers heavily devoted to one subject, only to make a complete turnaround after studying or even working in their initially chosen field. There is always time to reinvent yourself, develop new interests, or decide on a completely different academic route. There is time to embark on new friendships and relationships and learn from them, even if not all the people you meet end up forming part of your tribe.

In this book, I have shared what I consider to be the pillars of a happy school life. In chapter 1, we delved into Autism and the specific challenges it poses. With knowledge of how the Autistic brain works, parents, loved ones, and teachers can understand that when an Autistic child does not perform a task, it is because she cannot, not because she does not want to. Autistic girls face specific learning challenges that make it harder to perceive, process, and apply information. These challenges can not only affect her academic performance but also impact her self-esteem and the relationships she builds with others.

In Chapter 2, we investigated different options for schooling, including inclusion, special education, and even unschooling. There is no "best" option for everyone, so finding the right fit for your child will involve research, visiting schools, and discovering the extent to which your shortlist of schools can accommodate your child's needs. Next, in Chapter 3, we highlighted the importance of routines. Because transitions between activities and change can be so challenging for Autistic kids, it is important to harness the power of routines through visual schedules, social stories, and dedicated apps. All these tools help to let your child know what to expect to the greatest extent possible. Preparing your child as early as possible for upcoming changes is also key. There are many strategies you can use to make changes easier for her, including mindfulness meditation, breathing, and creating sensory and sleep "kits."

From chapters 4 to 6, we tackled specific obstacles your daughter may face in her school life, including learning, sensory, and social challenges. I highlighted the importance of personalized instruction that aligns with your child's learning style and interests. I also stressed the importance of enlisting the help of an occupational therapist to create a sensory map and share it with your child's teachers and school.

Throughout numerous chapters in this book, I shared numerous techniques, websites, and apps that can help your child achieve a sense of calm when sensory overload arises. Finally, I presented the main social issues your child may encounter at school, including pressure to mask and a lack of empathy from others. You saw that encouraging your child to join special interest groups, define and solidify her strawberry friendship group, and rely on siblings and family can all help her feel like part of something larger than herself.

This is undoubtedly a digital age, and that is why harnessing top technology can take you and your child far when it comes to achieving numerous goals. In chapter 7, I suggested apps for everything from learning to communication, sensory challenges, and mental health. Technology can help your child in many ways and provide a source of sensory relief. However, finding the right balance between screen use and outdoor and group activities is also key.

Throughout your daughter's childhood years, teaching her the techniques she needs to boost her resilience is key. There is so much that you can do to help her understand that she is perfect just the way she is. One of the most vital steps for building resilience is knowing how to set boundaries. I offered strategies that you can use to show your child that she is free to set boundaries in many aspects of her life—including how she spends her time, whom she shares her things with, and her wants, needs, and beliefs. To boost her confidence, it is equally important to exercise self-compassion, self-care, and self-acceptance. Tools like positive affirmations will help your child strive to align her actions with the things she believes in. In chapter 9, we delved into how to deal with the different stressors and anxieties that can impact your daughter's well-being at school. We saw how communication, a good relationship with your child's teachers, and proven natural anti-stress techniques can help her identify her triggers and regulate her emotions in her preferred manner.

Finally, we turned our eye to the future … to goals such as boosting your child's independence, preparing her for puberty, and getting her excited about college and career choices. We tapped into strategies that empower your child to be a strong self-advocate. We also gave you tips for planning her future for greater peace of mind.

Without a doubt, there are numerous goals to set and achieve. I suggest taking it one step at a time while also maintaining forward momentum. I hope that you celebrate every small achievement, not only those made by your child but also those that you make happen. You are your daughter's most powerful warrior. You are the one tasked with researching, calling professionals, meeting teachers … the person who tries to create a more empathetic world, one in which others make the effort to understand and know the wonderful person your daughter is. Best of luck with all your plans, and thank you for reading my words and the many testimonials of the wonderful Autistic girls and women who continue to inspire me every day.

HELP SOMEONE DARE TO DREAM BIG

Thank you for reading this guide to helping an Autistic girl live her fullest life during her school years. The many techniques I shared have been proven to be successful in various studies, but they also come from the many loving parents, teachers, and friends of Autistic girls. They have been an invaluable source of help throughout my research and writing process, and I'd like to thank every one of them for their heartfelt testimonials and recommendations.

If you're new to the Autism community, I hope that you are already excited about joining a support group, downloading useful apps, and planning a host of activities and projects you can undertake with your child. I can imagine that all these tasks will keep you super busy. Before you go, however, please do me a small favor. Take just half a minute to let other parents know where they can find the information they need to tackle the learning, sensory, and social challenges their child may face at school.

Scan the QR code below to leave your review.

Thanks for your support. I wish you and your child many opportunities to discover yourselves, tap into your passions, and create lovely memories together.

Taylor Eberstadt

ALSO BY TAYLOR EBERSTADT

Help your child hone her skills to achieve her goals, boost her self-esteem, and show her the power of unconditional love.

For too many years, Autism in children has been viewed from a male-centered lens.

Many girls are misdiagnosed with everything from BPD to multiple personality disorder—which creates great confusion for families and stops girls from receiving the right therapies early on.

This book, written by an Autistic teacher and mom, gives parents all the resources they need to spot the signs of Autism in girls so they can opt for diagnosis if they wish and make the best decisions regarding treatments.

In this book, you will discover:

- **Exactly what Autism is, how it affects skills like language and learning, and how it can look significantly different in girls than in boys**
- The pros and cons of early diagnosis—plus concurrent conditions that many Autistic girls face
- The reason Autistic girls have sensory issues and all **the powerful techniques you can use to reduce sensory overwhelm**

- Supporting your child's learning process—how to make learning fun and why supporting special interests is vital for her self-esteem and enjoyment
- How Autism affects communication and how you can **create a language-rich environment**
- Specialized coping strategies, calming tools, and exercises to **boost your daughter's emotional well-being**
- How to expand your daughter's opportunities to make friends —while prioritizing her specific wants and needs
- How to design Autistic-friendly sensory spaces in your home
- Why an accepting mindset is the most powerful tool against stigma and biases
- **A bonus chapter** on top professionals and current treatments that can support learning, sensory needs, and social skills

And much more.

Even if you already have a qualified and wonderful team, this book will empower you as a parent, highlighting the misconceptions to watch out for and presenting you with the latest research on approaches that work.

Nobody knows your child better than you. Get ready to be their strongest and most effective advocate!

Scan the QR code to find the book on Amazon.

REFERENCES

Abrams, Kelley Yost. n.d. "Exploring the Pros and Cons of an Autism Diagnosis." Jigsaw Diagnostics. Accessed December 21, 2024. https://www.jigsaw-dx.com/post/exploring-the-pros-and-cons-of-an-autism-diagnosis

Access Computing. n.d. "What Is an Individualized Education Plan?" Accessed January 7, 2025. https://www.washington.edu/accesscomputing/what-individualized-education-plan

Adey-Jones, Del. 2020. "Parenting Through the Principles." Medium. November 24, 2020. https://medium.com/less-stress-more-success/parenting-through-the-principles-7e44d322c062

Adina ABA. n.d. "Developing Consistent Routines to Empower Those with Autism." Accessed January 8, 2025. https://www.adinaaba.com/post/autism-routines

Advanced Autism Services. 2024. "Inspiring and Insightful Autism Quotes." November 19, 2024. https://www.advancedautism.com/post/autism-quotes

Alex Alexander. 2023. "Strawberry Friends: Forming Supportive Friendships While Neurodivergent." August 3, 2023. https://alexalexander.com/forming-supportive-friendships-while-neurodivergent/

Allstar ABA Therapy. n.d. "How Is Autism a Barrier to Learning?" Accessed December 21, 2024. https://www.allstaraba.org/blog/how-does-autism-affect-learning

Anti-Bullying Alliance. n.d. "Our Definition of Bullying." Accessed January 22, 2025. https://anti-bullyingalliance.org.uk/tools-information/all-about-bullying/understanding-bullying/definition

Apex ABA Therapy. 2024a. "Understanding Vestibular Stimming in Autism." December 12, 2024. https://www.apexaba.com/blog/vestibular-stimming-in-autism

Apex ABA Therapy. 2024b. "Sibling Responsibilities and Autism: How to Support a Brother or Sister?" June 16, 2024. https://www.apexaba.com/blog/sibling-responsibilities-and-autism

Apex ABA Therapy. 2024c. "5 Best Jobs for People on the Autism Spectrum." June 16, 2024. https://www.apexaba.com/blog/jobs-for-people-on-the-autism-spectrum?6b55a564_page=2

Apex ABA Therapy. 2024d. "20 Best Colleges for Autistic Students." June 6, 2024. https://www.apexaba.com/blog/colleges-for-autistic-students

Ashburner, Jill, Jenny Ziviani, and Sylvia Rodger. 2008. "Sensory Processing and Classroom Emotional, Behavioral, and Educational Outcomes in Children with Autism Spectrum Disorder." *American Journal of Occupational Therapy* 62 (5): 564–73. https://doi.org/10.5014/ajot.62.5.564

Attwood & Garnett Events. 2023. "Anxiety in Young Autistic Children: Part 2." December 14, 2023. https://www.attwoodandgarnettevents.com/blogs/news/anxiety-in-young-autistic-children-part-2

REFERENCES

Attwood, Tony. 2007. *The Complete Guide to Asperger's Syndrome.* Jessica Kingsley Publishers.

Autism Awareness Australia. n.d.-a. "Communication Challenges for Young Children." Accessed December 21, 2024. https://www.autismawareness.com.au/navigating-autism/communication-challenges-for-young-autistic-children

Autism Awareness Australia. n.d.-b. "Women and Girls." Accessed January 1, 2024. https://www.autismawareness.com.au/understanding-autism/women-girls

Autism Blog Treatment Center of America. 2023. "The Son-Rise Program Approach to Setting Boundaries with Our Children." March 17, 2023. https://blog.autismtreatmentcenter.org/2023/03/how-to-set-boundaries-with-our-children-in-a-son-rise-program-way.html

Autism Girls Network. n.d. "Autistic Girls Network Groups." Accessed January 13, 2025. https://autisticgirlsnetwork.org/face-to-face-groups/

Autism Speaks. n.d.-a. "What Is Autism?" Accessed December 21, 2024. https://www.autismspeaks.org/what-autism

Autism Speaks. n.d.-b. "Executive Functioning." Accessed December 21, 2024. https://www.autismspeaks.org/executive-functioning

Autism Speaks. n.d.-c. "Autism in Schools: Your Child's Rights." Accessed January 7, 2024. https://www.autismspeaks.org/autism-school-your-childs-rights

Autism Speaks. n.d.-d. "Seven Things to Know About Extended School Year (ESY) Services." Accessed January 7, 2025. https://www.autismspeaks.org/blog/seven-things-know-about-esy

Autism Speaks. n.d.-e. "Bullying Statistics and Facts." Accessed January 22, 2025. https://www.autismspeaks.org/bullying-statistics

Autism Speaks. n.d.-f. "Autism Diagnostic Criteria: DSM-5." Accessed January 22, 2025. https://www.autismspeaks.org/autism-diagnostic-criteria-dsm-5

Autism Speaks. n.d.-g. "Community-Based Skills Assessment (CSA): Developing a Personalized Transition Plan." Accessed January 24, 2025. https://www.autismspeaks.org/tool-kit/community-based-skills-assessment

Autism Specialty Group. n.d. "Understanding the Importance of Consistency in Autism." Autism Specialty Group. Accessed January 8, 2025. https://www.autismspecialtygroup.com/blog/importance-of-consistency-in-autism

Autism Teaching Strategies. 2014. "ASD CBT Video for Children Number 1." YouTube Video, 3:25. https://youtu.be/af04iwPN6vI?si=Y154J1Vktz9hsv4f

Autistic Girls at School. n.d. "Common Challenges at School." Accessed January 7, 2025. https://autisticgirlsatschool.com.au/CommonChallenges/InternalisingAndHiddenAnxiety

Autistic Girls Network. n.d. "Autism, Girls, & Keeping It All Inside." Accessed January 23, 2025. https://autisticgirlsnetwork.org/keeping-it-all-inside.pdf

Barker, Melissa, Rebecca Brewer, Jennifer Murphy. 2021. "What Is Interoception and Why Is It Important?" Frontiers. June 30, 2021. https://kids.frontiersin.org/articles/10.3389/frym.2021.558246

Berthold, Jess. 2024. "For Preteens, More Screen Time Is Tied to Depression, Anxiety Later." University of California San Francisco. October 7, 2024. https://www.ucsf.edu/news/2024/10/428581/preteens-more-screen-time-tied-depression-anxiety-later

Bestbier, Lana, and Tim I. Williams. 2017. "The Immediate Effects of Deep Pressure on Young People with Autism and Severe Intellectual Difficulties: Demonstrating Individual Differences." *Occupational Therapy International* 2017 (January): 1–7. https://doi.org/10.1155/2017/7534972

Bhavanani, Ananda Balayogi, Soccalingam Artchoudane, Meena Ramanathan, and Artchoudane Mariangela. 2019. "Yoga as a Therapeutic Tool in Autism: A Detailed Review." *Yoga Mimamsa* 51 (1): 3. https://doi.org/10.4103/ym.ym_3_19

Brickhill, Rae, Gray Atherton, Andrea Piovesan, and Liam Cross. 2023. "Autism, Thy Name Is Man: Exploring Implicit and Explicit Gender Bias in Autism Perceptions." *PLoS ONE* 18 (8): e0284013. https://doi.org/10.1371/journal.pone.0284013

Briot, Kellen, François Jean, Ali Jouni, Marie-Maude Geoffray, Myriam Ly-Le Moal, Daniel Umbricht, Christopher Chatham, et al. 2020. "Social Anxiety in Children and Adolescents with Autism Spectrum Disorders Contribute to Impairments in Social Communication and Social Motivation." *Frontiers in Psychiatry* 11 (July). https://doi.org/10.3389/fpsyt.2020.00710

Cailuns. 2024. "How to Build Self-Advocacy Skills in Your Autistic Child." Gersh Academy. April 8, 2024. https://www.gershacademy.org/blog/how-to-build-self-advocacy-skills-in-your-autistic-child

Calm. n.d. "5-4-3-2-1 Grounding: How to Use This Simple Technique for Coping with Anxiety." Accessed January 11, 2025. https://www.calm.com/blog/5-4-3-2-1-a-simple-exercise-to-calm-the-mind

Cardaro, Brett. 2023. "10 Things You Didn't Know About Satoshi Tajiri, the Creator of Pokémon." CBR. December 10, 2023. https://www.cbr.com/pokemon-creator-satoshi-tajiri-facts-into

Cardy, Robyn, Corinna Smith, Hamshi Suganthan, Zhuoran Jiang, Baiyu Wang, Mahan Malihi, Evdokia Anagnostou, and Azadeh Kushki. 2023. "Patterns and Impact of Technology Use in Autistic Children." *Research in Autism Spectrum Disorders* 108 (September): 102253. https://doi.org/10.1016/j.rasd.2023.102253

Cazalis, Fabienne, Elisabeth Reyes, Séverine Leduc, and David Gourion. 2022. "Evidence That Nine Autistic Women Out of Ten Have Been Victims of Sexual Violence." *Frontiers in Behavioral Neuroscience* 16 (April). https://doi.org/10.3389/fnbeh.2022.852203

Centre for Autism Middletown. n.d. "Proprioceptive." Accessed January 11, 2025. https://sensory-processing.middletownautism.com/sensory-strategies/strategies-according-to-sense/proprioceptive/

Cherney, Kristeen. 2024. "Alexithymia: Difficulty Recognizing and Feeling Emotions." Healthline. November 1, 2024. https://www.healthline.com/health/autism/alexithymia

Cherry, Kendra. 2023. "Gardner's Theory of Multiple Intelligences." Verywell Mind. March 11, 2023. https://www.verywellmind.com/gardners-theory-of-multiple-intelligences-2795161

Cherry, Kendra. 2024. "Exploring VARK Learning Styles: Which One Boosts Your

Learning Potential?" Verywell Mind. December 3, 2024. https://www.verywellmind.com/vark-learning-styles-2795156

Children's Hospital of Philadelphia. n.d. "Tools to Help with Stress: Progressive Muscle Relaxation." Accessed January 23, 2025. https://www.chop.edu/health-resources/tools-help-stress-progressive-muscle-relaxation

Cleveland Clinic. n.d. "Acceptance and Commitment Therapy (ACT)." Accessed January 8, 2025. https://my.clevelandclinic.org/health/treatments/acceptance-and-commitment-therapy-act-therapy

Common Sense Media. 2024. "4 Apps to Help Younger Kids with Self-Control." Understood. March 29, 2024. https://www.understood.org/en/articles/apps-to-help-younger-kids-with-self-control

Crompton, Catherine J., Sonny Hallett, Danielle Ropar, Emma Flynn, and Sue Fletcher-Watson. 2020. "'I Never Realised Everybody Felt as Happy as I Do When I Am Around Autistic People': A Thematic Analysis of Autistic Adults' Relationships with Autistic and Neurotypical Friends and Family." *Autism* 24, no. 6 (March): 1438–48. https://doi.org/10.1177/1362361320908897

Deolinda, Andréas. 2025. "Alexithymia and Autism: A World Without Emotions." Autism Parenting Magazine. January 5, 2025. https://www.autismparentingmagazine.com/alexithymia-autism/

Diff Not Less. 2023. "Empower Your Child with Autism: Unlocking the Power of a Growth Mindset." June 10, 2023. https://diffnotless.com/blogs/blog/teach-child-autism-growth-mindset

Dillon, Kelly. n.d. "Sensory Anxiety: Not Your Ordinary Anxiety." Accessed January 23, 2025. https://sensoryhealth.org/node/1129

Els for Autism. 2023. "30 Quotes from 30 People with Autism—The Sequel!" April 21, 2023. https://www.elsforautism.org/30-quotes-from-30-people-with-autism-the-sequel/

Embrace Autism. 2024. "Alexithymia & Autism Guide." July 21, 2024. https://embrace-autism.com/alexithymia-and-Autism-guide/

Erieau, Chelsea. 2019. "The 50 Best Resilience Quotes." Driven. February 20, 2019. https://home.hellodriven.com/articles/the-50-best-resilience-quotes/

Estes, Annette, Jeffrey Munson, Tanya St John, Robin Finlayson, Juhi Pandey, Bridget Gottlieb, John Herrington, and Robert T. Schultz. 2022. "Sleep Problems in Autism: Sex Differences in the School-Age Population." *Autism Research* 16 (1): 164–73. https://doi.org/10.1002/aur.2848

Fitzgerald, Natalie. 2023. "Understanding Autism Learning Styles: Differences, Tips and FAQs." Forbrain. September 4, 2023. https://www.forbrain.com/autism-learning/autism-learning-styles/

Friend in Me. n.d. "Connecting Kids with Disabilities and Neurotypical Students Through Online Games and Conversations." Accessed January 13, 2025. https://www.friendinmegroup.org/

Frothingham. 2024. "Musical Intelligence: Definition, Examples & Characteristics." Simply Psychology. February 2, 2024. https://www.simplypsychology.org/musical-intelligence.html

Funderstanding. 2024. "The Ultimate Guide for the Sequential Learners." June 19, 2024. https://funderstanding.com/teachers/the-ultimate-guide-for-the-sequential-learners/

Garey, Juliann. n.d. "The Controversy Around ABA." Accessed January 7, 2025. https://childmind.org/article/controversy-around-applied-behavior-analysis/

Gaydos, Ann. 2023. "First, Do No Harm: 'Unschooling' a Neurodivergent Child (Part 2)." Alliance Against Seclusion & Restraint. April 18, 2023. https://endseclusion.org/2023/04/18/first-do-no-harm-unschooling-a-neurodivergent-child-part-2/

Gehret, Melissa. 2020a. "Autism and Learning Disabilities." Spectrum of Hope. August 6, 2020. https://spectrumofhope.com/blog/Autism-and-learning-disorders/

Gehret, Melissa. 2020b. "Common Autism-Related Health Conditions." Spectrum of Hope. August 6, 2020. https://spectrumofhope.com/blog/common-health-conditions-that-co-occurr-with-Autism/

Goldstar Rehabilitation. 2023. "The Link Between Autism and Dyslexia: Explained." November 16, 2023. https://www.goldstarrehab.com/parent-resources/autism-and-dyslexia

Grandin, Temple. 1999. "Choosing the Right Job for People with Autism or Asperger's Syndrome." Indiana University Bloomington. November 1999. https://www.iidc.indiana.edu/irca/articles/choosing-the-right-job-for-people-with-autism-or-aspergers-syndrome.html

Grossman, Hallie. 2021. "An Introduction to CBT for People with an Autism Spectrum Disorder." Beck Institute. June 8, 2021. https://beckinstitute.org/blog/an-introduction-to-cbt-for-people-with-an-autism-spectrum-disorder/

Gunner, Elizabeth. 2015. "Questions to Ask on School Visits." Special Needs Jungle. February 20, 2015. https://www.specialneedsjungle.com/questions-ask-school-visits/

Guo, Xiaonan, Tiago Simas, Meng-Chuan Lai, Michael Lombardo, Bhismadev Chakrabarti, Amber Ruigrok, Edward T. Bullmore, Simon Baron-Cohen, Huafu Chen, and John Suckling. 2019. "Enhancement of Indirect Functional Connections with Shortest Path Length in the Adult Autistic Brain." *Human Brain Mapping* 40, number 18 (August): 5354–69. https://doi.org/10.1002/hbm.24777

Harvard Sleep Medicine. n.d. "Sleep and Mood." Accessed January 22, 2025. https://sleep.hms.harvard.edu/education-training/public-education/sleep-and-health-education-program/sleep-health-education-87

Healis Autism Centre. 2021. "Can Children with Autism Pretend Play?" July 13, 2021. https://www.healisautism.com/post/can-children-autism-pretend-play

helloEd. 2023. "Top 24 Technology Choices to Know About for Autism in 2023." April 5, 2023. https://www.helloedlife.com/post/top-20-technology-choices-helping-individuals-on-the-autism-spectrum-in-2021

Hendrickx, Sarah. 2015. *Women and Girls with Autism Spectrum Disorder: Understanding Life Experiences from Early Childhood to Old Age.* Jessica Kingsley Publishers.

Hogeveen, Jeremy, and Jordan Grafman. 2021. "Alexithymia." *Handbook of Clinical Neurology*, January, 47–62. https://doi.org/10.1016/b978-0-12-822290-4.00004-9

Hume, Kara, Rachel Loftin, and Johanna Lantz. 2009. "Increasing Independence in Autism Spectrum Disorders: A Review of Three Focused Interventions." *Journal of Autism and Developmental Disorders* 39 (9): 1329–38. https://doi.org/10.1007/s10803-009-0751-2

Iannone, Antonio, and Daniele Giansanti. 2023. "Breaking Barriers—The Intersection of AI and Assistive Technology in Autism Care: A Narrative Review." *Journal of Personalized Medicine* 14 (1): 41. https://doi.org/10.3390/jpm14010041

Jones, Carly. 2022. "Safeguarding Autistic Girls at School." National Autistic Society. May 5, 2022. https://www.autism.org.uk/advice-and-guidance/professional-practice/safeguarding-girls

Knickmeyer, Rebecca C., Sally Wheelwright, and Simon B. Baron-Cohen. 2007. "Sex-Typical Play: Masculinization/Defeminization in Girls with an Autism Spectrum Condition." *Journal of Autism and Developmental Disorders* 38 (6): 1028–35. https://doi.org/10.1007/s10803-007-0475-0

Kurcinka, Mary Sheedy. 2006. *Raising Your Spirited Child: A Guide for Parents Whose Child Is More Intense, Sensitive, Perceptive, Persistent, Energetic.* William Morrow Paperbacks.

Laber-Warren, Emily. 2021. "The Benefits of Special Interests in Autism." The Transmitter. May 12, 2021. https://www.spectrumnews.org/features/deep-dive/the-benefits-of-special-interests-in-autism/

Laurie, Corinna. 2022. "Ten Simple Sensory Strategies for Autistic Children." National Autistic Society. May 13, 2022. https://www.autism.org.uk/advice-and-guidance/professional-practice/sensory-strategies

Leclerc, Emily. 2024. "New Research First to Test 60-Year-Old Theory on Autism." Waisman Center. March 28, 2024. https://www.waisman.wisc.edu/2024/03/28/new-research-first-to-test-60-year-old-theory-on-Autism/

Leventhal, Barbara. 2024. "Choosing a Special School for Autism: 6 Important Factors to Consider." JRA Educational Consulting. February 9, 2024. https://www.jraeducationalconsulting.com/blog/choosing-a-special-school-for-autism

Libster, Natalie, Azia Knox, Selin Engin, Daniel Geschwind, Julia Parish-Morris, and Connie Kasari. 2023. "Sex Differences in Friendships and Loneliness in Autistic and Non-Autistic Children Across Development." *Molecular Autism* 14 (1). https://doi.org/10.1186/s13229-023-00542-9

LifeSpring Counseling Services. n.d. "How to Create a Sensory Tool Kit for Anxiety & Worry." Accessed January 12, 2025. https://lifespringcounseling.net/blog/sensory-toolkit

Living on the Spectrum. 2023. "Why Girls with Autism Face Unique Anxiety Challenges." May 21, 2023. https://www.livingonthespectrum.com/health-and-wellbeing/why-girls-with-autism-face-unique-anxiety-challenges/

Long, Caroline. 2024. "Procrastination or Learned Helplessness?" Elon Psychology. June 24, 2024. https://www.elonpsychology.com/blog/procrastination-or-learned-helplessness

Lumiere Children's Therapy. 2017. "Child Therapy: Proprioceptive Sensory Activities." May 15, 2017. https://www.lumierechild.com/blog/child-therapy-proprioceptive-sensory-activities/

Magro, Kerry. n.d. "10 Inspiring Quotes from People with Autism." Autism Speaks. Accessed December 21, 2024. https://www.autismspeaks.org/life-spectrum/autism-quotes

Matusiak, Manar. n.d. "24 Quotes from Autistic Individuals." Living Autism. Accessed January 8, 2025. https://livingautism.com/24-quotes-Autistic-individuals/

McCaffrey, Rachel Ferguson. 2018. "Reducing Anxiety in Autistic Children and Young People." National Autistic Society. April 5, 2018. https://www.autism.org.uk/advice-and-guidance/professional-practice/anxiety-parental

McHugh, Stephen. 2024. "Autism and Learning How to Do Laundry." Stephen's Evolution. May 21, 2024. https://stephensevolution.com/autism-and-learning-how-to-do-laundry/

Medcalf, Laura. 2017. "7 Apps to Help Calm Individuals with Autism, Anxiety, Other Special Needs." Easterseals Crossroads. April 19, 2017. https://www.eastersealstech.com/2017/04/19/chill-outz-relaxation-techniques-children/

Meyer, Sara. 2024a. "Friendship May Look Different for Autistic People." Altogether Autism Takiwatanga. March 4, 2024. https://www.altogetherautism.org.nz/friendship-may-look-different-for-autistic-people/

Meyer, Sara. 2024b. "Autism and Social Anxiety." Altogether Autism Takiwatanga. May 14, 2024. https://www.altogetherautism.org.nz/autism-and-social-anxiety/

Misheva, Emilia. 2024. "Autism and Girls: Friendships and Relationships." The British Psychological Society. September 4, 2024. https://www.bps.org.uk/psychologist/autism-and-girls-friendships-and-relationships

Montaser, Jamal, Lotanna Umeano, Hari Priya Pujari, Syed Muhammad Zain Nasiri, Anusha Parisapogu, Anuj Shah, and Safeera Khan. 2023. "Correlations Between the Development of Social Anxiety and Individuals with Autism Spectrum Disorder: A Systematic Review." *Cureus*, September. https://doi.org/10.7759/cureus.44841

Moore, Catherine. 2019. "Positive Daily Affirmations: Is There Science Behind It?" Positive Psychology. March 4, 2019. https://positivepsychology.com/daily-affirmations/

Moore, Debra. 2023. "Simple Ways to Avoid 'Learned Helplessness' with Autism." Autism Parenting Magazine. October 12, 2023. https://www.autismparentingmagazine.com/simple-ways-avoid-learned-helplessness-Autism/

Morin, Amanda. n.d. "7 Tips for Talking to Your Child's Teacher About Sensory Processing Challenges." Understood. Accessed January 11, 2025. https://www.understood.org/en/articles/sensory-processing-challenges-talking-to-teachers

Mulligan, Emily. n.d. "Ten Ways to Build Independence." Autism Speaks. Accessed January 24, 2025. https://www.autismspeaks.org/tool-kit-excerpt/ten-ways-build-independence

Must, Aviva, Misha Eliasziw, Heidi Stanish, Carol Curtin, Linda G. Bandini, and April Bowling. 2023. "Passive and Social Screen Time in Children with Autism and in Association With Obesity." *Frontiers in Pediatrics* 11 (July). https://doi.org/10.3389/fped.2023.1198033

National Autistic Society. n.d.-a. "What Is Autism?" Accessed December 21, 2024. https://www.autism.org.uk/advice-and-guidance/what-is-autism

National Autistic Society. n.d.-b. "Exams—A Guide for Parents." Accessed January 10, 2025. https://www.autism.org.uk/advice-and-guidance/topics/education/exams/parents

National Autistic Society. n.d.-c. "Anxiety." Accessed January 23, 2025. https://www.autism.org.uk/advice-and-guidance/topics/mental-health/anxiety

Neff, Megan Anna. n.d. "Autism and Alexithymia: Similarities, Differences, and Overlap." Neurodivergent Insights. Accessed January 20, 2025. https://neurodivergentinsights.com/blog/autism-and-alexithymia

NHS Essex Partnership University. n.d. "Sensory Processing in Learning." Accessed December 21, 2024. https://eput.nhs.uk/patient-carer-and-visitor/children-and-young-people-experiencing-sensory-processing-needs/sensory-processing-in-learning/

North Shore Pediatric Therapy. 2024. "Creating SMART Goals for Kids with Autism." February 1, 2024. https://www.nspt4kids.com/healthtopics-and-conditions-database/autism-spectrum-disorder/creating-smart-goals-kids-autism

Notbohm, Ellen. 2022. *Ten Things Your Student With Autism Wishes You Knew*. Future Horizons.

NPR. 2022. "Devon Price on Self-Acceptance for People with Autism." August 9, 2022. https://www.npr.org/2022/08/03/1115469855/devon-price-on-self-acceptance-and-expression-for-people-with-autism

O'Connor, Rachel A.G., Neeltje Van Den Bedem, Els M.A. Blijd-Hoogewys, Lex Stockmann, and Carolien Rieffe. 2022. "Friendship Quality Among Autistic and Non-Autistic (Pre-) Adolescents: Protective or Risk Factor for Mental Health?" *Autism* 26 (8): 2041–51. https://doi.org/10.1177/13623613211073448

Otsimo. 2023. "Deep Pressure Therapy for Autism." September 28, 2023. https://otsimo.com/en/deep-pressure-therapy-autism/

Outschool. n.d. "Complete Guide to the 4 Learning Preferences and 8 Intelligences." Accessed January 19, 2025. https://outschool.com/articles/4-learning-preferences-8-intelligences?

Palmer, Ann. n.d. "Strategies for Surviving Middle School with an Included Child with Autism." Accessed January 24, 2025. https://pathfindersforautism.org/articles/education/strategies-for-surviving-middle-school-with-an-included-child-with-autism/

Papyrus. n.d. "The Importance of Setting Boundaries and Saying No." Accessed January 22, 2025. https://www.papyrus-uk.org/setting-boundaries/

Pathways.org. n.d. "What Is Proprioception? Understanding the 'Body Awareness' Sense." Accessed January 11, 2024. https://pathways.org/what-is-the-proprioception-sense/

Paulise, Luciana. 2023. "How to Use the Power of Self-Compassion to Manage Perfectionism." Forbes. July 25, 2023. https://www.forbes.com/sites/lucianapaulise/2023/07/25/how-to-use-the-power-of-self-compassion-to-manage-perfectionism/

Pellicano, Liz and Felicity Sedgewick. 2017. "Friendships Pose Unique Challenges for Women on the Spectrum." The Transmitter. May 16, 2017. https://www.thetransmitter.org/spectrum/friendships-pose-unique-challenges-women-spectrum/

Penot, Jessica L. 2023. "The Problematic Issues of Boundaries and Autism." Psychology Today. January 14, 2023. https://www.psychologytoday.com/intl/blog/the-forgotten-women/202301/the-problematic-issue-of-boundaries-and-autism

Piller, Aimee, and Joseph Barimo. 2019. "Sensory Strategies to Calm and Engage Children with Autism Spectrum Disorder." *ASHA Leader* 24 (4): 56–63. https://doi.org/10.1044/leader.ftr2.24042019.56

Powers, Annette. 2013. "Slow Days, Fast Years." Huffpost. July 24, 2013. https://www.huffpost.com/entry/young-children-divorce_b_3328030

Price, Devon. *Unmasking Autism: Discovering the New Faces of Neurodiversity*. Arlington: Future Horizons Inc., 2022.

Raising Children. n.d.-a. "Siblings of Autistic Children and Teenagers: Experiences, Relationships and Support." Accessed January 13, 2025. https://raisingchildren.net.au/autism/communicating-relationships/family-relationships/siblings-asd

Raising Children. n.d.-b. "Bullying: Autistic Children and Teenagers." Accessed January 22, 2025. https://raisingchildren.net.au/autism/behaviour/common-concerns/bullying-asd#if-the-bullying-doesnt-stop-nav-title

Raising Children. n.d.-c. "Learning About Bodies and Personal Boundaries: Autistic Children." Accessed January 22, 2025. https://raisingchildren.net.au/autism/development/physical-development/bodies-boundaries

Raising Children. n.d.-d. "Circle of Friends: Personal Boundaries Activity for Children 3–15 Years." Accessed January 21, 2025. https://raisingchildren.net.au/autism/development/sexual-development/circle-of-friends-personal-boundaries-activity-children-3-15-years

Raising Children. n.d.-e. "Sensory Integration Therapy." Accessed January 23, 2025. https://raisingchildren.net.au/autism/therapies-guide/sensory-integration

Raising Children. n.d.-f. "Social Anxiety in Children." Accessed January 23, 2025. https://raisingchildren.net.au/toddlers/health-daily-care/mental-health/social-anxiety

Raising Children. n.d.-g. "Periods: Preparing Autistic Children." Accessed July 24, 2025, https://raisingchildren.net.au/autism/development/physical-development/periods-and-autism

Rawe, Julie. 2024. "The Difference Between IEPs and 504 Plans." Understood. May 18, 2024. https://www.understood.org/en/articles/the-difference-between-ieps-and-504-plans

Reed, Steph. 2022. "Emotional Regulation: Teaching Autistic Kids to Recognise Their Emotions." Autism Spectrum Teacher. December, 2022. https://autismspectrumteacher.com/emotional-regulation-teaching-children-autism-recognise-respond-emotion/

Reframing Autism. n.d. "Milton's 'Double Empathy Problem': A Summary for Non-Academics." Accessed January 23, 2025. https://reframingautism.org.au/miltons-double-empathy-problem-a-summary-for-non-academics/

Ricciardi, Courtney, Olga Kornienko, and Pamela W. Garner. 2022. "The Role of Cognitive Emotion Regulation for Making and Keeping Friend and Conflict

Networks." *Frontiers in Psychology* 13 (April). https://doi.org/10.3389/fpsyg.2022.802629

Riis, Kathryn, Brittany Samulski, Kristina A. Neely, and Patricia Laverdure. 2024. "Physical Activity for Anxiety for Autistic People: A Systematic Review." *Journal of Autism and Developmental Disorders*, May. https://doi.org/10.1007/s10803-024-06356-9

Rivera-Bonet, Charlene N. 2023. "Sensory Responses in Autistic Children Are Linked to a Small Under-Explored Region Tucked Deep Down in the Brain Called the Brainstem." Waisman Center. April 5, 2023. https://www.waisman.wisc.edu/2023/04/05/sensory-responses-in-Autistic-children

Rowley, Emma, Susie Chandler, Gillian Baird, Emily Simonoff, Andrew Pickles, Tom Loucas, and Tony Charman. 2012. "The Experience of Friendship, Victimization and Bullying in Children with an Autism Spectrum Disorder: Associations with Child Characteristics and School Placement." *Research in Autism Spectrum Disorders* 6 (3): 1126–34. https://doi.org/10.1016/j.rasd.2012.03.004

Rudy, Lisa Jo. 2023. "Assistive Technology for Autism." Verywell Health. November 8, 2023. https://www.verywellhealth.com/assistive-technology-for-autism-5076159

Rudy, Lisa Jo. 2024a. "8 Types of Schools for Autistic Kids." Verywell Health. October 3, 2024. https://www.verywellhealth.com/educational-options-for-children-with-autism-260393

Rudy, Lisa Jo. 2024b. "Apps for Autism." Verywell Health. July 11, 2024. https://www.verywellhealth.com/apps-for-autism-4768574

Santa Barbara Estate Planning & Elder Law. n.d. "5 Estate Planning Tips for Families with Children on the Autism Spectrum." Accessed January 25, 2025. https://www.sbelderlaw.com/estate-planning-tips-for-parents-with-autistic-children/

Sarris, Marina. 2018. "Anxiety's Toll on People with Autism." Kennedy Krieger. January 3, 2018. https://www.kennedykrieger.org/stories/interactive-autism-network-ian/anxietys-toll-people-autism

Sattayakhom, Apsorn, Sineewanlaya Wichit, and Phanit Koomhin. 2023. "The Effects of Essential Oils on the Nervous System: A Scoping Review." *Molecules* 28 (9): 3771. https://doi.org/10.3390/molecules28093771

Schulze, Sarah. 2022. "The Importance of a Bedtime Routine for Children with ADHD." Joon. October 24, 2022. https://www.joonapp.io/post/bedtime-routine-for-children-with-adhd

Sedgewick, Felicity, Laura Crane, Vivian Hill, and Elizabeth Pellicano. 2019. "Friends and Lovers: The Relationships of Autistic and Neurotypical Women." *Autism in Adulthood* 1 (2): 112–23. https://doi.org/10.1089/aut.2018.0028

Sedgewick, Felicity, Vivian Hill, and Elizabeth Pellicano. 2018. "'It's Different For Girls': Gender Differences in the Friendships and Conflict of Autistic and Neurotypical Adolescents." *Autism* 23 (5): 1119–32. https://doi.org/10.1177/1362361318794930

Seppala, Emma. 2014. "The Scientific Benefits of Self-Compassion." Stanford Medicine. May 8, 2014. https://ccare.stanford.edu/uncategorized/the-scientific-benefits-of-self-compassion-infographic/

Silvertant, Eva. 2020. "Alexithymia & Autism Guide." Embrace Autism. January 27, 2020. https://embrace-autism.com/alexithymia-and-autism-guide/

Sousa, David A. 2016. *How The Brain Learns.* Corwin Press.

Spain, Debbie, Jacqueline Sin, Kai B. Linder, Johanna McMahon, and Francesca Happé. 2018. "Social Anxiety in Autism Spectrum Disorder: A Systematic Review." *Research in Autism Spectrum Disorders* 52 (May): 51–68. https://doi.org/10.1016/j.rasd.2018.04.007

Special Strong. n.d. "4 Best Calming Exercises for Sensory Overload and Meltdowns." Accessed January 11, 2024. https://www.specialstrong.com/4-best-calming-exercises-for-sensory-overload-and-meltdowns/

Sturrock, Alexandra, Helen Chilton, Katie Foy, Jenny Freed, and Catherine Adams. 2021. "In Their Own Words: The Impact of Subtle Language and Communication Difficulties as Described by Autistic Girls and Boys Without Intellectual Disability." *Autism* 26 (2): 332–45. https://doi.org/10.1177/13623613211002047

Swain, Deanna. 2022. "Practice Mindfulness to Reduce Stress." Organization for Autism Research. January 4, 2022. https://researchautism.org/oaracle-newsletter/practice-mindfulness-to-reduce-stress/

Takarae, Yukari, and John Sweeney. 2017. "Neural Hyperexcitability in Autism Spectrum Disorders." *Brain Sciences* 7 (10): 129. https://doi.org/10.3390/brainsci7100129

TEACCH® Autism Program. n.d. "About Us." Accessed January 24, 2025. https://teacch.com/about-us/

The Autism Helper. n.d. "Focus on Five: Teaching Self-Compassion." Accessed January 22, 2025. https://theautismhelper.com/focus-on-five-teaching-self-compassion/

The Autism Project. n.d. "Social Groups." Accessed January 13, 2025. https://theautismproject.org/parents-families/programs-resources/social-groups

The Spectrum. n.d. "Disability Support Worker for Autistic People." Accessed January 24, 2025. https://thespectrum.org.au/autism-support-services/professionals/disability-support-worker-for-people-with-autism/

Thompson, Dennis. 2023. "Kids with Nonverbal Autism May Still Understand Much Spoken Language." Medical Xpress. May 4, 2023. https://medicalxpress.com/news/2023-05-kids-nonverbal-autism-spoken-language.html

Tippett, Krista. 2015. "Brené Brown: The Courage to Be Vulnerable." On Being. January 9, 2015. https://onbeing.org/programs/brene-brown-the-courage-to-be-vulnerable-jan2015/

Twinkle. n.d. " 7 Autism Awareness and Acceptance Quotes to Use in the Classroom." Accessed February 18, 2025. https://www.twinkl.es/blog/7-autism-awareness-quotes-to-use-in-the-classroom

UCLA Health. 2022. "Brain Changes in Autism Are Far More Sweeping than Previously Known, UCLA-Led Study Finds." November 2, 2022. https://www.ucla-health.org/news/release/brain-changes-Autism-are-far-more-sweeping-previously-known

Undivided. 2024. "What Qualifies a Student for a 1:1 Aide or Other Paraeducator."

October 23, 2024. https://undivided.io/resources/what-qualifies-a-student-for-a-1-1-aide-or-other-paraeducator-206

van der Cruijsen, Renske, and Bianca E. Boyer. 2020. "Explicit and Implicit Self-Esteem in Youth with Autism Spectrum Disorders." *Autism* 25 (2): 349–60. https://doi.org/10.1177/1362361320961006

Wassner, Jodie. n.d. "ACT with Young People on the Autism Spectrum." Contextual Consulting. Accessed January 23, 2025. https://raisingchildren.net.au/autism/therapies-guide/sensory-integration

Waterhouse, Lynn. 2023. "Why Multiple Intelligences Theory Is a Neuromyth." *Frontiers in Psychology* 14 (August). https://doi.org/10.3389/fpsyg.2023.1217288

Weiner, Luisa, Madalina Elena Costache, Doha Bemmouna, Juliette Rabot, Sébastien Weibel, Marine Dubreucq, Julien Dubreucq, and Romain Coutelle. 2023. "Emotion Dysregulation Is Heightened in Autistic Females: A Comparison With Autistic Males and Borderline Personality Disorder." *Women's Health* 19 (January): 174550572311747. https://doi.org/10.1177/17455057231174763

Wingert, Shawna. 2024. "5 Powerful Ways to Teach Growth Mindset to Children with Special Needs." Big Life Journal. July 4, 2024. https://biglifejournal.com/blogs/blog/growth-mindset-children-special-needs-adhd-autism

Wirecutter. 2024. "The Best Parental Control Apps to Manage Screen Time (and Keep Your Kid Safer Online)." December 18, 2024. https://www.nytimes.com/wirecutter/reviews/best-apps-to-manage-your-kids-phone/

Yacoub, Amy. 2023. "Is Your Child a Gestalt Language Processor?" Therapy Works. March 10, 2023. https://therapyworks.com/blog/child-development/gestalt-language-processor/

Yau, Natalie, Sonia Anderson, and Ian C. Smith. 2023. "How Is Psychological Wellbeing Experienced by Autistic Women? Challenges and Protective Factors: A Meta-Synthesis." *Research in Autism Spectrum Disorders* 102 (January): 102101. https://doi.org/10.1016/j.rasd.2022.102101

Yellow Bus ABA. 2024. "Best Autism Quotes to Raise Awareness and Understanding." October 2, 2024. https://www.yellowbusaba.com/post/autism-quotes

Zurich. 2023. "10 Ways to Boost Your Personal Resilience and Better Cope with Stress." April 11, 2023. https://www.zurich.com/media/magazine/2021/10-steps-that-will-increase-your-personal-resilience

www.ingramcontent.com/pod-product-compliance
Lightning Source LLC
Chambersburg PA
CBHW031248290426
44109CB00012B/480